PETER VANDENBERG
WITH TANYA GARDINER

Into the Unknown

RECKLESSLY
FOLLOWING THE CALL OF
GOD

FOREWORD BY
REINHARD BONNKE

CfaN CHRIST
FOR ALL NATIONS

Australia • Brazil • Canada • Germany • Hong Kong • Singapore

DEDICATED TO

Evangeline Elizabeth Vandenberg

I dedicate this book to my wife, the love of my life, my best friend, my confidante and partner, the mother of my children, who has walked this long and sometimes uncertain road with me but has never hesitated nor held back.

TABLE OF CONTENTS

FOREWORD

THE PEARL IN THE OYSTER

Wow. What a wonderful book. Jesus spoke of the "pearl of great price" in a different context, but in Peter Vandenberg's book, I found a beautiful pearl in an oyster. He shares how he and his wife Evangeline probed their trust in Jesus, long before our ways intertwined. It is a life story that glorifies Jesus most wonderfully.

I met Peter for the first time in 1980 in the City Hall of Birmingham, England, and we ministered the Gospel together. When he told me after the service that the Holy Spirit had spoken to him to join CfaN, I was puzzled and replied, "*We do not need another preacher in the ministry; we may need perhaps a mechanic for our fleet of cars and trucks.*" A highly qualified minister become a mechanic? He told me of his elaborate engineering qualifications – and we shook hands on it. Although many opposed, Peter and family came back to Africa.

At every team meeting when problems had to be solved and Peter spoke up, he had a good solution. A few months later, Peter became our General Manager and my right-hand man in teaching and preaching the Gospel. I honor him for listening to the Holy Spirit, for his humility, loyalty and obedience. He was at my side until I retired and is now at the side of my successor, Daniel Kolenda. Peter's share of ministry empowered through the Holy Spirit, is immense.

When I heard about Peter's love for hang gliding, I became concerned and thought it was too risky. Our ministry motto is "*Africa shall be saved.*" I was in China when I heard he had crashed and broken his neck. God answered prayer in a miraculous way, but I told Peter, *"Please, no more hang gliding before Africa is saved."*

The epic of a blood-washed Africa continues with combine harvesters speeding along – and people getting saved. Peter and Evangeline are among them. They will not finish, but complete the race, to the glory of God the Father.

Reinhard Bonnke
Evangelist, Founder of Christ for all Nations

INTRODUCTION

Peter was born in 1947 in Zimbabwe, then called Rhodesia. He obtained diplomas in automotive engineering and aviation engineering from the City and Guilds of London. In 1969, he married Evangeline Raper and they have three children, six grandchildren and one great grandchild. By the age of 26, he rose to the position of Managing Director in the family business, served on the church board of his local fellowship and led the youth work. He and Evangeline answered the call of God to full-time service in 1974, which resulted in them going, with their three young children, to Elim Bible College in England for a three-year course. Early on, they launched a music ministry, singing and preaching at hundreds of churches a year, while completing their studies.

Peter pursued varied studies, both through the Bible college and at other institutions, gaining Diplomas in Theology and Public Speaking from Elim Bible College, the University of London and The New Era Academy of Arts and Drama, London.

He completed the five-year term of service for ordination with the Elim Pentecostal Church in England and has held credentials with them since 1975.

After seven years of evangelistic ministry with the Gospel singing group Rufaro, he joined Evangelist Reinhard Bonnke at Christ for all Nations (CfaN) in 1981. He has worked in this ministry full-time since then and has been instrumental in building the work up from early beginnings to the present day. Peter currently serves as Executive Vice President of CfaN, now incorporated in ten countries worldwide. He has preached in

CfaN Fire Conferences since their inception, speaking face-to-face to millions of leaders and pastors.

He lives with his wife, Evangeline, near the CfaN USA office in Florida. Peter is still fully engaged in and committed to the ongoing ministry of CfaN under the leadership of Daniel Kolenda, having been involved in piloting the succession of Daniel to leadership before and after Reinhard's retirement.

He has been an enthusiastic hang glider pilot for over 40 years now, is an advanced Scuba Rescue diver, and enjoys boating, fishing and extreme off-roading. But he always says,

"The greatest adventure of my life has been to follow the call of God."

The Publisher

PROLOGUE

Into the jaws of the lion

I squeezed the light aircraft down through the only hole in the solid overcast sky, desperate to get below the clouds to establish visual contact with the ground below. I was lost, far from home and low on fuel. It was an international flight in our small single-engine mission plane, and I was on the way from one country to another when an instrument failure meant that I could no longer navigate without fixing our position visually. For that, I needed to see the earth below.

The little plane popped through the hole in the clouds and we levelled out below the low cloud base. I was relieved to see the ground again, but the satisfaction was short-lived when I realized that nothing below us was familiar to me at all. I had no idea where we were, but I knew one thing for sure. We only had an hour and fifteen minutes of fuel left in the tanks.

This well-intentioned mission trip had suddenly gone very wrong, and my heart raced as adrenaline kicked my brain into survival mode. We droned on over vast expanses of trackless bush, my eyes darting between the unfamiliar scenery and my now-useless maps. I was hoping and praying for some recognizable feature to tell me where we were. Flying low to stay beneath the clouds, we suddenly zoomed over a grass landing strip. My heart raced with excitement as I said to my passenger, "Werner, we'll continue for ten minutes and if I still don't know where we are, we'll come back to land here and ask!"

Landing during an international flight is not permitted – but this was an emergency.

We were soon back over the grass landing strip and I was preparing to land. I buzzed low over the landing area to chase the grazing cows away, routine practice in bush flying, but I was puzzled by the fact that the cows didn't move, and no one appeared to herd them.

"We'll have to land in the short part of the runway before the cows," I said to Werner. "And tighten your seatbelt. This may get rough!"

With the plane safely down, I taxied back to the start of the runway, ready for an immediate takeoff, and we climbed out. Seemingly out of nowhere, scores of young African children appeared and Werner, as was his custom in children's ministry, hauled balloons out of his pocket and began blowing them up and handing them to the kids. They squealed and shouted as they reached for the balloons and then, as one boy took his balloon, I heard him say, "Muito obrigado," which is "thank you" in Portuguese.

My heart sank, and I felt a cold shiver run down my spine. I realized in that instant that we had landed in the country of Mozambique, not only way off our intended course, but a country locked in a bitter and vicious civil war. I looked up and shivered again as I saw a band of 'comrade soldiers' walking toward us from the nearby bush. They carried AK47 assault rifles at the ready, with bandoliers of ammunition around their necks.

I knew we were in trouble.

We had landed at a military garrison in the remote north of the country and to make matters worse, we were in a South African-registered aircraft, which I knew would not be well received. South Africa, at that time, was assisting the rebel army against the communist government forces. As I walked towards the soldiers, I breathed a silent prayer.

"Lord, we need your help – *now*!"

How did I get myself into this situation in the first place?

PART 1

The Journey of a Lifetime

"For I know the plans I have for you," declares the LORD, "PLANS TO PROSPER YOU AND NOT TO HARM YOU, PLANS TO GIVE YOU HOPE AND A FUTURE."

Jeremiah 29:11

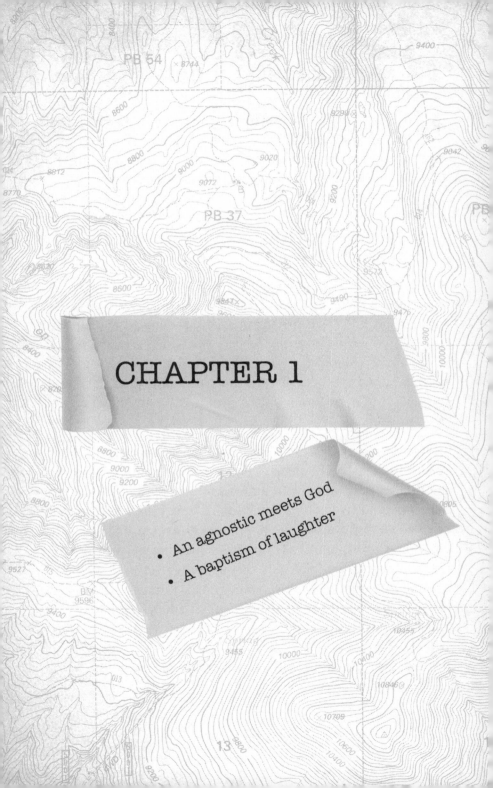

CHAPTER 1

- An agnostic meets God
- A baptism of laughter

An agnostic meets God

Nothing of my childhood in the sleepy, sun-baked backwater of Zimbabwe gave any hint of future adventures and global travel in the pursuit of God's calling. Like any little boy in a tropical country, my days were spent finding new ways to torment my two older sisters, and happily shooting things with my trusty rubber catapult. Home, in Harare, was a happy, stable place, our needs well met by industrious parents who labored to build a successful motoring business and a comfortable family life.

There was plenty to do for a boy who loved all things mechanical, and I was driving at age 10 (sitting on an empty oil can to see over the steering wheel) and soon tinkering on cars of my own. Technical school and an apprenticeship as a motor mechanic had me on a steady track to working in the family business, but in one important aspect I was determined to walk my own path.

Ours was a typical church family, with parents who faithfully served in their local Pentecostal assembly. My mom, Alice, ran the Sunday school and had a finger in practically every church pie. Dad (known to all as 'Uncle Japie') was the vice-chairman of the church for many years, holding down the fort as pastors came and went, and was a devoted member of the Gideons. Church was an integral part of our lives. But as I grew into adulthood, I rejected the Christian message. It was full of holes, in my opinion, and I had great difficulty with the conflict of faith and reason. It seemed perfectly obvious to me that the faith I witnessed around me was unreasonable, and I became not only a firm agnostic, but a gleefully active one, an anti-evangelist with an axe to grind.

Flexing my intellectual muscles, and armed to the teeth with a solid doctrinal arsenal from years of church, I liked nothing more than arguing Christians under the table. I still maintained many Christian friends, but as far as I was concerned, none of them had the guts to ask the hard questions I was tackling, and which the Christian faith - I felt - could not answer. And so I went my own way, crafting an airtight personal philosophy that seemed unchallenged by those I presented it to.

As the years went by, this neatly packaged agnosticism became firmly entrenched, and I thought it unshakable. It wasn't as though I felt any great need for God anyway, since I had my own life nicely in hand. By now I was running Matthews Garage with my father and enjoying life thoroughly, with motor racing on the weekends and plenty of friends to drink with. There didn't seem to be anything missing, but unbeknownst to my oblivious young self, God was quietly working in the background, and was about to get my attention.

Way down South, in the city of Johannesburg, my sister, Louise, was staying with family friends. I'd met Pastor Oliver Raper's gorgeous daughter, Evangeline, when she visited Harare with her family some years before. I was 18, she was 19, and after making hopeful eyes at her, I'd said to Louise, "If she'll wait for me to grow up, I'm going to marry her!" Now, three years later, this paragon of beauty and intellect was on her way to surprise me on my 21st birthday. My teenage self's saucy pronouncement turned out to be prophetic, and we quickly fell in love. Many eagerly-awaited letters, long-distance calls and expensive plane trips later, we were engaged.

For the life of me, I don't know why this pastor's daughter, herself a Christian who loved the Lord deeply, was willing to commit to a life with an outspoken agnostic. She says she knew from the start that I would ask her to marry me, and that she would say yes. Nevertheless, my heathen state was of deep concern to her, and she wrote a heartfelt letter to me, saying, "How can you commit to me, a frail human being, and not commit yourself to God?" I replied, "I can see you. I can't see God!" But, thank the Lord, she stuck with me and began praying fervently, not knowing that she was joining my mother's faithful intercession of many years.

No doubt the Lord knew that the one thing a young man in love with a beautiful woman cannot do, is to say no! So, when Evangeline called to say that some friends, a couple newly returned from Bible school in the States, were coming to Harare, and asked me to go and support them at the local church where they were preaching, I didn't hesitate.

"Sure!" I said, "Why not?" I still had Christian friends, amazingly, and I wasn't against going along for a midweek meeting. Anything to please 'Evangeline-the-Favorite'!

Off I duly went, to the homey, very traditional Pentecostal church, with long wooden pews and orange-tinted windows. It was all familiar to me, having grown up there, knowing all the faces. Jannie Pretorius, the newly-minted preacher, got up and spoke about Samson, and how he went against God's plan. I listened, mentally tearing holes in the sermon as he spoke, dismantling the message, as was my way, chuckling inwardly at the philosophical mistakes that seemed obvious to me. Then he turned it into a Gospel message and gave an altar call.

"Yup, that's standard practice," I thought. "Pulling on the emotional strings now." I wasn't antagonistic, just pretty sure I knew what the lay of the land was; their good old church tactics were not fooling me.

The sermon was finished, and I was more than ready to leave, but the preacher kept going on and on with the altar call. It was getting uncomfortable, and I thought, "What's wrong with this guy? Can't he see nothing's going to happen?"

Up at the front, Jannie persevered; "I'm not going to close this altar call. You need to come forward. You need to kneel here and receive Jesus." Moments stretched into awkward minutes, and I checked surreptitiously from side to side, but nothing was happening, and he just would not stop. What was this guy's problem? Enough already! "You need Jesus. Come to the front and receive Jesus as your Lord and Savior," he insisted.

Eventually, it started to get through to me. Something inside me said, "Go on and do it," and my horrified response was, "No way!" I broke out in a cold sweat and shuffled nervously in my seat, drumming my fingers on the pew in front of me. And then I just couldn't stand it anymore. To my own surprise, my internal voice said, "I'm going to do it!" I jumped up, went straight to the front, and knelt at the altar. Instantly, I burst into tears, crying like a baby, which was not my style at all. Where was this coming from? What on earth was happening?

Jannie knelt to pray with me, and I didn't notice a thing as the church quietly emptied behind me. After a while, my tears dried, and I walked out into the night, by now alone, and utterly bemused. I couldn't fathom what had happened, and told myself that I'd surely be okay in the morning. Why I should have had such an emotional outburst, I could not explain, but I was quite sure that a good sleep would take care of it. But morning came, and I was not "okay." I was not "normal." It wasn't that I was unhappy – in fact, I was *really* happy. But I felt different. Something fundamental had changed inside me, and my philosophy could not explain it. I had no answer, and I couldn't argue it away, as I was wont to do with doctrinal questions, because I could *feel* that something inside me was different.

"Well, it's emotionalism," I thought, but that didn't hold water, because there I was, sitting at breakfast and not feeling emotional at all. As the day went by, and that feeling remained, I realized that something in my spirit had truly changed. How could that be? I didn't change myself. That change must have come from outside of me. God was not the disinterested, somewhere-out-there entity of my agnostic philosophy. God, for reasons yet unknown to me, was interested enough to reach out and change the heart of an unbelieving young man, in a little old church, in an ordinary town, deep in Africa.

Days went by, and it became clear that this change, this deep-down shift in my spirit, was here to stay. That understanding crumpled my agnostic philosophy, because I had experienced something that I could not explain away or even begin to quantify. I couldn't shake it, because it was real. "I was wrong," I thought, "God is real, and He does reach out and touch us. And if I was wrong about that, what else am I wrong about?"

Of course, I had to tell Vangi (my pet name for Evangeline), and I sat down to write a letter, since international phone calls cost a fortune back then. Still not comfortable with saying something as Christian as "I got saved," I started my letter with, "I must eat humble pie, because something has happened that I can't explain…" The Lord surely heard her prayers, because three months later, she walked up the aisle to wed – not an agnostic – but a young man now committed to her and committed to serving Jesus.

A baptism of laughter

That first year of following Jesus was a busy one, between getting married to Evangeline, running the family business and being thrown in the deep end at church. Our pastor had no qualms about putting a new convert to work, and before long, I was on every church committee but the ladies' group. While I was perfectly happy being of service as the youth leader, I remained a quiet, reserved person in the services. While Vangi privately and fervently prayed for God to move my heart and do something for me, I felt I barely deserved to be included. After all, I had spent years actively arguing against the Word of God, delighting in breaking down people's faith. I felt I really didn't have the right to be joyfully praising along with other, better Christians.

I can see now that much of this was a young man's pride, but at the time, I had once again rationalized my relationship to God. My reserved demeanor in church I attributed to being like my introvert father. This went on for about a year, until Vangi and I went to the annual church camp, a 5-day event deep in the bush at Macheke. In between the camp-style meetings, many an hour was spent sitting around the fire, talking in depth about God, praying for one another, and experiencing the move of the Holy Spirit together. That was something I was present for, yet separate from.

Then one evening, a well-known guest speaker by the name of PD Le Roux launched into his message without the customary scripture reading. "You are the righteousness of God!" he thundered, and he held forth on this topic with gusto for a while. "What nonsense," I thought, listing to myself all the bad that I had done, all the arguing and the running away and the persecuting of others. "This is blasphemy! This is rubbish! He can't say that. It just isn't true!" But then he pulled out his Bible, and delved into the message, fully backed up with chapter and verse, showing how grace, grace and only grace presents us as the righteousness of God in Christ Jesus.

I was deeply rattled by this message, so directly in conflict with my false humility. Vangi could tell from my body language that I was upset, even angry. After the meeting, with this powerful word buzzing in my head and stirring up my spirit, I sat near the fire again, thinking about the preacher's words. Others were praying for each other, ministering in the Holy Spirit and laying hands on one another. Right there, I made a simple decision; to take part, to get involved, to hold back no longer.

Immediately, the power of the Holy Spirit fell on me, and I was flat on my back on the grass, laughing and laughing and laughing. I laughed for two hours, so hard that my stomach muscles were stiff the next day. When friends asked me later what I was laughing at, I told them as much as I could remember. "The devil! I was laughing at the devil!" The devil would fool me no more with his lies of inadequacy and guilt.

From that moment on, my life was changed forever. No more quietly going with the flow. Now I was filled with the joy of the Lord, baptized in the Holy Spirit and eager to hear from God. I went from being content with the ordinary to leaping into "life more abundantly." The adventure of a lifetime, of recklessly following the call of God, had just begun.

CHAPTER 2

- It seemed good to us
- That "cheesy" feeling
- Off to Bible college

It seemed good to us

I have many times been asked what the most exciting thing is that I've ever done. Given my love of adventure, sports and flying, I think people usually expect an answer that includes plenty of adrenaline and a cliff or two! But I always answer, "Following the call of God." That has been the driving force in my life, taking me to places and into situations that I would never have had the imagination to think up for myself. Thank God, He gave me a partner to go adventuring with, my beautiful and talented wife, Evangeline. It's worth taking a moment to look at how we began to hear the voice of God for ourselves, since everything else that followed in our lives comes back to this process.

In the early days of our marriage, while I was working in the family business and serving on one church committee after another, Evangeline was creating a home for our growing family; first, a little girl, Tanya, swiftly followed by a son, Gregory, and then another boy, Courteney. As happy as we were together, and as much as we enjoyed the normal triumphs of young family life, we were also challenged and intrigued by the possibilities of a life really lived in faith.

What would that even look like? How was it possible to hear from God, and to figure out what God's plan was for our lives? We were certainly inspired by other young people we knew, who had 'heard the call of God' and gone off to distant countries to learn how to be ministers. In addition, we had the example of Vangi's parents, living out the call in their own lives as full-time pastors in Johannesburg. What about us? What did God want of us and our little family?

When you're eager to hear from God, He is more than willing to give you opportunities to learn to recognize His voice. God knows better than to start us off with the big stuff. He speaks into our hearts, and as we act in obedience, our faith is built. At first, it was as simple as being obedient in tithing our income and following other principles that are clearly written in the Bible. Then we started to look beyond that, wondering what God's plan might be for our lives. I wondered, *"How do I know if God is speaking to me? How do I hear God's voice for myself?"*

Other people that I knew talked so easily about hearing from God. *"How does that even work?"* I thought. *"Do they actually hear a voice? Is it a feeling? How do they know it's God that's speaking?"* And on top of that, well-meaning Christians were constantly telling me, much to my annoyance, that there was a call on my life. I wondered how they could know that if I didn't even know it myself?

Then I found myself reading in Acts 15 about the apostles and elders sending some chosen men out to minister in Antioch, and I was riveted by these words:

> *"... it seemed good to us, being assembled with one accord, to send chosen men to you with our beloved Barnabas and Paul," (Acts 15:25 NKJV) and then again later, "For it seemed good to the Holy Spirit, and to us ..." (Acts 15:28 NKJV)*

It *seemed* good to them?! They weren't even really sure, but they went out, and the work was blessed. I could certainly relate to that. If something seemed good to me, and the Holy Spirit was involved, I was willing to give it a go. That thought stayed in my mind, on the back burner, for a while.

There was a couple in our church, Roy and Val, who were roughly our age. Roy was a banker, and if I had given it any thought at all, I would have said they were in the same income bracket as we were, and probably better off. One Sunday morning, as I was loading the stroller and baby bag into the car, getting ready to leave for church, I had a sudden feeling, an odd sensation in my belly.

By now, I had almost forgotten about 'it seemed good,' but here came this strong impression that I should give Roy $20. It seemed good to me for a moment, and then the internal argument started. *"Is this a good idea? Surely not. It's such a small amount of money. What could he possibly want with $20? If I do this, I'll embarrass him. And I'll look stupid. This is a dumb idea."* But I couldn't shake it, and it still 'seemed good' to me. I went so far as to take $20 out of my wallet and put it in my pocket for easy access, just in case.

When we got to church, I saw Roy and Val sitting across the aisle, and I made up my mind to give him the $20 after all. The service ended, but by the time I'd navigated the hub-bub of greeting people and herding children, and looked around to find them, they were gone. No Roy and Val. *"Ah well, it was a silly idea anyway,"* I thought, and frankly, I was rather relieved. It had seemed good, but it wasn't to be. Vangi and I started loading the kids and stroller into the car, and then I realized I'd left my Bible in the building. I ran back to get it, grabbed it from the pew and turned around to leave. And there was Roy! He'd forgotten something too. In a millisecond, the choice was there. Did I want to try this or not? I did. I crumpled up the $20 note in my hand, still embarrassed by the smallness of the gift, and stuck my hand out.

"Roy, I feel I should give this to you."

Looking nonplussed, he put out his hand. I dropped the crumpled bill in it, turned around and walked away.

"Pete!"

I spun around to see Roy looking down at the bill, tears in his eyes. I hurried back to him.

"Pete, why did you do this?" he asked.

"Well, it seemed like the right thing to do," I said.

Tears were streaming down his cheeks now.

"Val and I are facing a huge decision right now, and I know I shouldn't ask for a sign, but that's exactly what I did this morning. I said 'Please, Lord, let something really unusual happen in church this morning, something that's never happened before.' And here you walk up to me and give me $20."

By now, there were tears in my own eyes, and as I walked back to the car to tell Vangi what had happened, I thought, "So that's how it works with me – a funny feeling in my gut and *'it seems good.'*" That 'silly' little gesture turned out to be a confirmation to Roy and Val to go to Bible college, which they duly did. It was no small thing to them, and it was a pivotal moment for me. God's ways are not our ways, and He sees far beyond our tiny understanding of what is small, what is great, and what makes a difference. There's no other way to move in the great call of God but to learn to trust His voice, and simply do what He says.

That "cheesy" feeling

As I began to experiment with prayer and listening to God, I discovered that I would always get that funny feeling in my belly when the Holy Spirit was trying to get my attention, an actual physical sensation that my family knows as 'that cheesy feeling,' since it reminds me of indigestion! I'm sure it's different for everyone and that there are many people whose direct line to God sounds a lot more spiritual than that, but that's just how it is with me and the Lord. When the Holy Spirit is nudging me, I get that odd cheesy feeling in my gut, and I've learned to pay attention.

Vangi and I started to test this business of hearing the voice of God, and our faith grew as we obeyed the Lord in giving bigger and bigger amounts of money where we felt Him directing us, each time seeing confirmation that we had correctly discerned the will of the Lord. It was exciting to be on this journey, and I thought I was really getting the hang of this listening thing, when suddenly, in 1974, our family business faced a crisis.

Zimbabwe – still known as Rhodesia then – was under UN sanctions. That had hurt us when we tried to turn the family business, a public company, into a private company. We had one shareholder in England, and as we were not allowed to do business with him, our plans were on hold. To our joy, the UN declared a two-week amnesty of the sanctions, and this was the chance for Vangi and me to buy back the shares for the sum of $5000, which was all our savings and about two years' salary.

My parents were on their way to the USA for a Gideons conference, leaving me, their young son and junior director of the company, to complete this crucial task. No problem! I knew I had it all in hand. We informed the lawyer of our plans, and we were ready. Then, just before the two-week window of opportunity opened, we found ourselves at church, listening to our local missionary, Willard Wilson, giving an update on the Bible school he was building.

"We're almost done, praise the Lord! But we've run out of funding to finish the roof. We're trusting the Lord for $5000 to get the job done."

Oh no! I had that all-too-familiar, too-much-cheese feeling in my stomach. The Holy Spirit was speaking to me. I tried to ignore it. $5000! *"No, no, this is different; this is too much. Come on, Lord."* But the feeling wouldn't leave, and I knew I had to obey. With no checkbook on me, I made a plan, and ripped out an empty page from the back of my Bible, writing 'Pete & Vangi – IOU $5000'.

The last hymn of the evening had barely stopped playing before Willard stood in front of me, holding that piece of paper. The check was in his hand the next day. I wasn't too worried. I figured I could simply get a loan from the bank for the shares, since our business was successful and stable. Imagine my horror when an apologetic bank manager explained that he couldn't issue a loan to me, the junior director, without my parents' signature. And they were somewhere in America!

The lawyer phoned to remind me that the window was opening the next day, and though I assured him that the sale was going ahead, I had no way of scraping the money together. Four days went by, and he phoned again to point out that he needed a whole week to put the transfer through. "It's coming. I'm on it," I said, but I knew I had exhausted every option. With my heart in my shoes, I started rehearsing my speech to tell my folks I had messed up this golden opportunity, that I had simply *given* the money away, like an idiot. I couldn't help but feel this 'leading of the Holy Spirit' thing was nonsense after all, and had just gotten me into a mountain of trouble.

And then a letter arrived from the IRS. I didn't want to open it – that was all I needed, on top of this mess, a tax demand from the IRS. I opened it warily, and my jaw dropped as I read that there had been 'irregularities' with my tax returns for the past four years, and enclosed was a check for $5000! No less and no more, exactly the amount needed to put the trade through. I phoned the lawyer, hurried over, and couldn't resist saying to him, "I know you're in a hurry, so here's a government banker's check!" The job was done. Vangi and I were over the moon, rejoicing at this amazing, clear proof of God's leading. Could there be anything bigger than this? Had we reached the apex, the epitome of awesome faith moments in our lives?

Off to Bible College

It wasn't more than a couple of months later that another visiting preacher stopped by our church. He preached from Hosea about 'breaking up your fallow ground,' and likened that ground, full of weeds and tares, to the mission field. In those days, there was a prevailing negative attitude toward missionaries, who were often considered the also-rans of ministry, the 'failed' pastors and evangelists. However, this preacher made it clear that God needed the best and brightest on the mission field, and that He was calling on people 'right in this room' to go into full-time ministry.

Sure enough – and by now you've guessed it – I felt that unmistakable feeling in my belly, and I knew the Holy Spirit was speaking to me. His voice had become familiar to me, and I knew that I had to stand up in answer to this call. As I stood, Vangi looked at me, stood up and took my hand. Who was the preacher, that momentous day? Amazingly, it was none other than Reinhard Bonnke, then a fiery young missionary – but it would be years before our paths crossed again.

The very next morning, we went to see our friend Willard, himself a great visionary, who encouraged me to speak to my parents. My dad was semi-retired by now, and I was the managing director of the business. How would they take the news that we wanted to go into full-time ministry? My mom said, without hesitation, "That's wonderful!" But what about my dad? A quiet man, very sparing with his words, he thought for a moment.

"I'd like to tell you a story," he said. "A long time ago, I felt God calling me to go into ministry. But I said, 'I've got a wife and children, and I don't have enough money to do that.' So, I thought I'd change my business to something that made a lot more money, tobacco farming."

I had never even heard about this before. It was news to me. He carried on:

"The first crop failed. And then the second crop. And then the third, and I sold up and came back to start my motor business up again. And I never went into ministry, because I didn't make the money. Don't you make the same mistake."

I was both dumbfounded and mightily encouraged. Vangi and I began to make plans in earnest. We immediately set about selling off everything we had; business shares, our house, our boat and our car. I worked out that we could just about afford three full years of college. Everyone else we knew who had gone into ministry had gone to Bible college in America, so we set our sights on the same. I wrote an enthusiastic, heartfelt letter to a highly-respected institution in the States, telling of how we had heard the call of God, and wanted to come to Bible School. And oh yes, I had a wife and three small children, and they were certainly going with me.

When I received a personal answer from the dean herself, it was not what we had hoped for. Words to the effect of 'you need to seriously re-evaluate what you think you've heard... you're irresponsible... a man with three children doesn't go to Bible school...' and so on. This put a damper on our dreams for a moment. But Vangi was having none of it.

"The woman's a fool. God has spoken to us, and we're going. Only not to that college!"

Just to please my father-in-law, I had also sent an application off to Elim Bible College in England, a college I'd never even heard of, and sure enough, just two days after that rejection, their acceptance letter arrived. They'd never had anyone with children attend before either, but their warm response was simply, "Come, and we'll figure something out!" That was good enough for us. England it would be.

Before long, with a mountain of luggage and three small children in tow (the youngest was only 10 months old) we set sail from Durban on the Windsor Castle, one of the last of the famous old Union Castle line. We arrived in Southampton on a cold, wet and windy day in September 1975, and the weather itself – so different from the pleasant tropical climate of Zimbabwe – was a good indicator of just how much our lives were about to change.

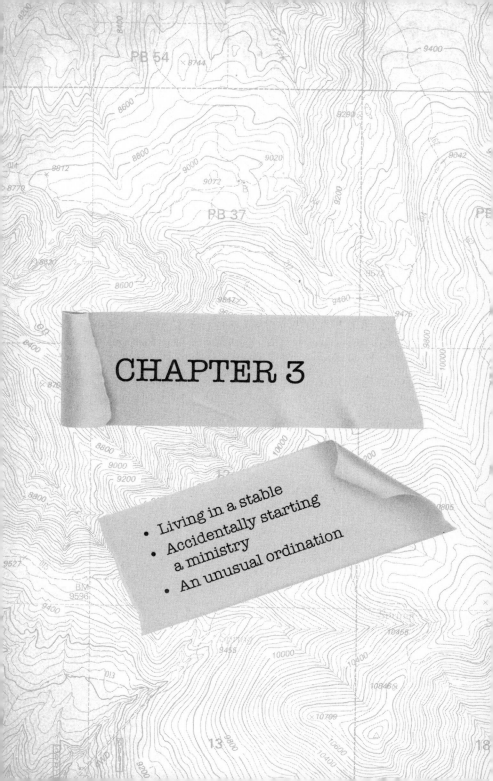

CHAPTER 3

- Living in a stable
- Accidentally starting a ministry
- An unusual ordination

Living in a stable

True to their word, the administrators of Elim Bible College had indeed found a solution for our family. Since it was impossible for us to join the other students in their dorms and shared rooms, they'd found a cottage on the grounds of Pleystowe House, once a stately home, and now used by the college as accommodation for students from all over the world. 'Cottage' is a kind word for what was actually a converted 400-year-old stone stable, complete with a stable door and a chimney that was made for horse-shoeing, and therefore efficiently funneled practically all heat straight through the roof.

It was astonishingly damp (we once came home to find mushrooms growing in the middle of the lounge floor) and sometimes colder than the inside of our refrigerator. We even had to bath our toddlers in a plastic tub in front of the fire, because the bathroom was so icy. Still, we were thrilled just to be there, and Vangi set about turning it into a welcoming, cozy home, a talent she has that's worked miracles many, many times in so many new places over the years.

Absolutely everything was new and different to me. The college was based in a glorious old mansion, like something from the movies, with its wooden paneling, Victorian-era bathrooms and magnificent gardens. England itself was another world, far more foreign than I had imagined, since we all spoke English, and I was from a former British colony after all. But there was no time to worry much about the cultural side of things. I threw myself immediately into student life and took as many courses as possible, always aware that the money we had was only enough for three years. Whatever was offered, I was eager to give it a go. That's how I ended up studying for several diplomas at once, including a diploma of Theology from the University of

London, a diploma of arts and drama from the New Era Academy of London as well as further qualifications from Elim.

There was still time for being young and having fun, of course. As a keen angler, I always enjoyed fishing and wondered if I would find a good place to fish here in these British Isles. During those early years at Bible school, many wonderful relationships were made, one of them with a student by the name of Anthony Kelton who became a lifelong friend.

He was also an angler and in response to my enquiry, he informed me that he had found a suitable fishing spot, so we loaded our fishing rods and set off to try our luck. We arrived at a remote, flooded quarry, apparently well known for record-size fish. As we approached the designated fishing site, I noticed a prominent sign standing in the water which very clearly said 'No Fishing.'

When I questioned the presence of the sign, Anthony's firm and instant reply was, "You foreigners worry about everything! This is England, Peter, just focus on your fishing."

Well, fish we did, and with some luck too. After about two hours of this bliss, I looked up and - to my horror - saw two fishermen approaching. They were dressed in the correct fishing gear, carrying rods and heading quite deliberately and intentionally towards us. I drew Anthony's attention to the approaching interruption, commenting that it looked like our fishing was over. He replied, "Peter, you just be quiet and leave this to me. I'll handle it."

When they were quite close to us, Anthony suddenly turned and walked very purposefully towards them with his fishing rod in his hand and I heard him addressing them directly.

"And what do you want here?" he asked.

I was amazed to see their demeanor instantly change. They answered very politely.

"We wanted to fish, if we may?" Anthony responded very firmly,

"Can you not read? The sign says NO FISHING!"

They immediately apologized profusely, turned around and walked quickly away. Anthony returned to the fishing and not a word was said between us, but I was greatly impressed.

We returned many more times to our favorite fishing spot and the episode of the 'hopeful fishermen' was repeated four or five times over. Each time the prospective fishermen would arrive while we were there, they would approach, Anthony would do his 'Lord of the Manor' presentation and they would respond in the same apologetic way, before quickly departing.

One day we were again fishing, and as it happens, I'd managed to land a record-sized fish which was securely tethered in anticipation of feeding the whole family later. I then looked up and on the other side of the quarry, I saw a very official-looking man with a somewhat large German Shepherd dog straining on a leash, approaching us purposefully. I realized immediately that he was the Game Warden, and he was obviously very interested in meeting up with us.

Not a word was said between Anthony and myself but as the warden and his dog came closer and closer, I said to Anthony, "I can't wait to hear what you are going to say to the dog!"

No further words were exchanged but with the warden and his dog now looking very alert and getting closer by the second, I saw Anthony jump into action, gathering up his gear while calling out urgently, "Let's go... NOW!"

I grabbed the evening dinner and my gear, and both of us headed out across a wheat field running as fast as our legs could carry us. We never looked back and never went back either. My only regret was that I never did find out what he was going to say to the dog.

Accidentally starting a ministry

The first year flew by, complicated by the sadness of losing my beloved mom to cancer. Being there in her last days meant flying all of us home and back, a significant strain on our carefully worked out budget. In addition to that, we had come face-to-face with a challenge we had heard of but completely failed to understand – the English winter. Back in Africa, we hadn't really had to heat anything, since winter was brief and mild. Now, not even the fun of seeing snow for the first time could make up for the daunting bills we faced to buy fuel for the hungry fireplace.

To supplement the expensive coal we were burning, I would chop up fallen trees from the grounds the cottage was on, heading to the woodshed most mornings with Aristotle – a tame pheasant we rescued – keeping me company. But no matter how much I chopped, the ever-shrinking woodpile was a clear indication that we would be running out of money a lot sooner than the three years we'd planned for.

By now, we had also been joined by Vangi's youngest brother, Oliver Raper. He'd just been on a year-long tour of the USA, traveling and performing with gospel singer Phil Enloe. Since he was on his way back to South Africa, and would have to stop in Europe anyway, it seemed a no-brainer to invite him to stay with us for a couple of months. He'd never seen England either, and he took us up on the offer immediately.

The visit turned into a permanent arrangement, once he decided to finish his half-done theology degree at Elim. It was inevitable that this would quickly result in a great deal of music being made, since Evangeline and Oliver had grown up in a family where singing around the piano was the order of the day. I also loved to sing, and we would spend hours making music as Vangi played, working out three-part harmonies to all the gospel favorites we loved so much.

I can't say if we were any good at the time, but we were certainly very loud – loud enough that other students heard us singing and took it on themselves to put us forward for the end-of-year entertainment at the college gala. It was a challenge we happily accepted, and we put many hours of practice into those three songs. Though we didn't yet have a name, that was the beginning of our gospel music ministry.

When we received an enquiry from someone wanting to book us, we settled on 'Rufaro,' a Shona word from Zimbabwe that loosely translates as 'joy and peace.' It gave us a feeling of being connected to our African home. Our first professional gig (that may be something of an overstatement) was for a working men's club. They may have misunderstood who we were, since they were thoroughly surprised at the gospel songs that came their way, performed with gusto on their very own honky-tonk piano in a smoke-filled, beer-sticky room!

It wasn't long before other more suitable bookings started coming our way, churches who had heard about us by word of mouth, and asked us to come and minister. We always saw the music as an important tool, a way of attracting people and getting their attention, to make way for the Word of God. Oliver and I were both fledgling preachers, and we took turns following the music with a brief message, a call to salvation.

From the very beginning, we as Rufaro asked ourselves how we should approach the matter of payment, because there were many costs involved in getting to the churches who invited us. In line with all that the Lord had been teaching us about the leading of the Holy Spirit and depending in faith on Him for all our needs, we came to the decision that we would never charge a fee. If anyone invited us, we would go, and we would trust God to pay our way.

This was considered extremely odd and unfeasible by pretty much everyone we knew in England. "That will never work here," we heard more than once. "Maybe in America, but that sort of thing just doesn't work in England." Nevertheless, we knew we had to be obedient to that still small voice, and so we told each church that we went to that we would accept whatever the Lord laid on their hearts to give us. As we'd often say, "We are here because of the last church that blessed us, and you're blessing the next church we go to."

Within just a few months, the number of bookings had grown so much that we were ministering practically every weekend, and not just in our local area. In fact, we were traveling to and fro in every direction, sometimes very far and for very little. On one memorable occasion, we drove an exhausting six hours, and when it came time to leave, the pastor handed us £10 and a bottle of jam! Though things like that happened now and then, there was never any doubt that God had it all fully under control, and the overall balance sheet was skewed in our favor. Very often, it was the smallest congregations that surprised us with their loving generosity.

We were soon able to replace our rusty and very overloaded little Anglia with an ancient, but much bigger, red Bedford van. This meant we could transport our growing pile of technical gear, as well as our children, who accustomed themselves to sleeping on top of speakers and cables. Rufaro was very much a family adventure, and when they weren't in school, the kids were part and parcel of everything we did.

We certainly hadn't planned on starting a Gospel music ministry, and could not have imagined it as a potential solution to our study money running out, or as a stepping stone to further ministry in the distant future. It was an accident, an accident of faith. We were already in the right place, having followed God's calling to Bible school. Sometimes, His leading is by the 'squeezing' of our circumstances, pushing us in one direction or another. There's nothing to fear about that, because when we're already headed in the direction He wants us to go, it's an easy matter for Him to nudge us to wherever else He wants us to be. I think this is also a classic example of how God uses our passions and interests to further His kingdom.

We didn't start Rufaro because we needed an income. We started Rufaro because we loved singing, and couldn't help doing it! The hours and hours that we spent working out harmonies and practising songs were for the love of it. Of course, when the ministry took off, then we had to work hard on our skills, but it was something we were already committed to. Our passions, our interests, the things we're good at, the things we love doing and can't stop telling people about – these are almost always good indicators of how God wants to use us. There's no great mystery to it. God made us in the first place, and He knows the desires of our hearts, and longs to bring us into excellence.

As it turned out, the tools we needed to see us financially through the last year of college, after our budget had run out, were already in our hands. Rufaro began to take on a life of its own. We started out as full-time students and part-time music ministers. By the final year, we were full-time ministers and part-time students! Thank God for the energy of the young, because we certainly needed it. Evangeline had taken on a faculty role as Director of the busy college choir, and I was Head Student. We had a family to look after, I had a full study load and external exams to write for my theology degree, and Rufaro somehow did over 400 gigs in that last year. Every moment was taken, and we had already set the pattern for the next few years, traveling to a different church every weekend to sing and preach multiple times.

An unusual ordination

The aim of finishing Bible College was, of course, to be ordained, and therefore licensed to minister. The usual plan – and in fact the mandatory policy – in the Elim denomination, was for newly graduated students to be sent out to spend two years as a youth pastor or assistant pastor. After five years, they received their ordination as *pastors*. Oliver, who was a year ahead of me, did go and spend a year as an assistant pastor, while continuing to minister with us in Rufaro. As for me, by the time the final year of college was over, Rufaro was already a full-blown, full-time ministry with bookings many months in advance, and we simply flowed from college directly into that ministry.

By the time I was to be ordained at the annual church conference two years later, we'd been traveling all over Great Britain, ministering in literally hundreds of churches, and we were well-known. When the conference rolled around, Rufaro was booked to minister, to lead the praise and worship and sing during services. Two days before the big ordination celebration, I was asked to come to a meeting of the curatorium. Here sat the leaders of the denomination, and it was clear they were in something of a quandary.

"Uh, Peter, if you could please take a seat. We have something of a problem. I'm afraid we won't be able to put you forward for ordination."

This came out of nowhere. I was completely taken by surprise.

"Why?" I asked. "What have I done?"

"No, no, it isn't you. It's just that one of our districts has filed a complaint. They say it goes against the Elim constitution to ordain someone who's never been a pastor. And the thing of it is, you see… they're right. So terribly sorry."

"Well, is there anything you can do?" I asked.

"Sadly, no, we won't be able to ordain you."

That seemed to be that, then. Had God led me wrong? Was going to Bible College a waste of time? In the years that Rufaro had been ministering, we had covered the length and breadth of the country. In time, we would visit literally every town, every city and every county in the whole of Great Britain. We knew that God was both leading us and blessing us. How could this refusal be part of His plan, when we *knew* that we were in the right place, doing exactly what God wanted of us?

The very next day was the ministerial conference, and the long list of names of those to be ordained was read to the gathered pastors and leaders. Mine was missing.

"… and one name is not being put forward for ordination, and that is Peter Vandenberg," said the speaker.

There was a moment of shocked silence, and then a growing murmur of voices. The vast majority of the pastors present had invited us to their churches in the last few years. We had stayed in their homes, joined them in evangelistic ministry, helped them bring in new members, and ministered to their flocks. We had sung with them, prayed with them, journeyed with them. Several voices yelled out from the crowd.

"Why?"

"What's the reason?"

The speaker lost no time in making it perfectly clear. This was not a case of bad morals or questionable doctrine.

"So-and-so from such-and-such district has brought it to our attention that it is unconstitutional to ordain someone who has never been a pastor."

There was a growing murmur of disbelief and dissent, and then people started jumping up all over the hall.

"Change it! We want this changed immediately!"

Someone else jumped up and managed to get everyone's attention.

"I put a motion forward, that this meeting is NOT closed, and the matter of changing the constitution so that Peter Vandenberg can be ordained must be brought to the General Council tomorrow, and we will meet afterwards to ratify it."

There was a roar of approval from the pastors! The following day, with the correct protocols observed, Elim changed their constitution to allow the ordination of people who are not pastors. It was a pioneering moment, and it paved the way for people with ministries in music, intercession, youth work and much more. On the final night of the conference, it was my turn to be called to the stage, and the entire executive leadership laid hands on me and ordained me for the Lord's work, whatever He might call me to do!

CHAPTER 4

- Singing the Gospel
- Recording albums
- A fresh call of God
- Any questions?

Singing the Gospel

During our final year at Bible school, Oliver was serving as assistant pastor in Chelmsford, a somewhat bleak industrial town in Essex, so we moved there as soon as college was done. All we could afford at the time was a tiny semi-detached row house, a 'two-up, two-down' that we proceeded to stretch to the limit. Vangi and I took the lounge, Oliver and his new bride, Brigitte, took the main bedroom, and we needed the tiny second bedroom for the young lady who looked after our children during school terms. That left nowhere for the three kids, but after some creative DIY, we somehow carved a space for them upstairs, an odd L-shaped room with triple bunk beds that I made from wooden doors. It was ridiculously tight, but it worked, and we set about building the ministry from there.

Rufaro already had bookings a full year in advance. With the number of miles we were doing, we soon upgraded our transport to a bigger, fancier white Mercedes van with our name on it, which we transformed to accommodate both our technical gear and our kids. Invitations came streaming in from churches across the length and breadth of the UK, and we settled into a rhythm, traveling to a new church almost every week, holding outreach meetings and ministering to congregations over the weekends.

Early on, just after we'd arrived to sing and preach at a church in Liverpool, the pastor took us aside and asked if we would be willing to sing at a local school assembly, with the hope of getting some of the young people to attend the nightly outreach meetings. We were eager to give it a try, and the next morning we set up speakers at an ungodly early hour, bleary-eyed and yawning. We did that a few times, but it wasn't having the desired effect, and seemed like a lot of effort with no return.

We were about to give up on schools altogether when a teacher at one of the schools approached us. "Would you consider rather coming to sing to the kids at lunch time?" she asked. It was a sixth form college, and lunch was an hour long. Unlike during assembly, when students were forced to be in the hall, this was unstructured time, with everyone milling around. We agreed, and duly arrived at one o'clock.

There were five teachers waiting for us. We later learned they weren't there to hear us sing but to protect us, as the school kids had the reputation of being extremely rough and unruly. Knowing nothing of that, we set up our gear, picked our most lively song and turned the volume up. Within moments, the hall began to fill with curious students, and when the teachers saw that we had the situation nicely in control, they quietly drifted away.

By the time the hour was nearly over, the hall was packed with hundreds of young people, and though we were nothing like the punk bands they loved so much (it was the 70's in England, after all) we seemed to have everyone's attention. We were building a great rapport, responding to some good-natured heckling, and getting laughs and applause back. Normally, we would finish off an outreach like this with a short Gospel message. But this was a public school, and technically, we were not supposed to do any preaching. Still, with no teachers around, it seemed a pity not to seize the opportunity.

"I don't know why I'm even telling you this," I said from the stage. "There's probably no-one here brave enough to stand out from the crowd and do something about it. But I'm going to tell you anyway!" I gave a very brief message, and without expecting much, called on those who wanted to give their lives to Jesus to come forward. The response was incredible, as many of these supposedly 'hard' Liverpudlian kids pushed their way to the front, leaning on the stage and bowing their heads as we led them in a salvation prayer.

When the teachers came back to see where their students were, there we were, praying with numerous kids, some of them crying, listening as they poured out their broken hearts to Jesus. When one teacher called out, "Where is my Physics class?" a young man yelled back, "Forget physics! This is more important!" God was working.

That evening, as we prepared for the week-night meeting in the little church we were visiting, I took the pastor aside.

"Look, I think you'd better prepare for a big influx of young people tonight."

"Really? Do you really think so?"

He looked rather skeptical, since church was the last place you'd find that disillusioned punk generation in. But he let the deacons and elders know, and when the doors opened, the church was indeed filled with rambunctious young people who'd freshly met Jesus that very day. It was a turning point for that church and for our ministry. From then on, we'd be sure to ask each pastor if there was a sixth form college nearby, and spent our lunch times singing and inviting young people to church.

Three years after that first Liverpool experience, Rufaro was singing at a large church event in the Royal Albert Hall in London. On stage was an enormous choir made up of people from Elim churches all over England. At the end of the evening, as we were packing up and rolling cables on the stage, three young women came over to talk to us. "Do you remember us?" one of them asked. I couldn't honestly say that I did. She went on, "You came to our school in Liverpool, and we all gave our lives to Christ that day." Then they told us that after we had been there, they had started having Bible studies at school, and became part of that local church. They had been serving Jesus faithfully ever since. To God be the glory!

Recording albums

In our second year of Bible college, Rufaro had come to the notice of Christian record producers Marshall, Morgan and Scott, who had a local label, Pilgrim Records. When they asked if we'd be interested in recording an album, we jumped at the chance, and off we went to their Eastbourne studio. We spent three days recording our first album, titled simply 'Rufaro,' on state-of-the-art 4-track tape. Over the next couple of years, we would record two more albums, upping our budget and production value each time, and buying our own stock to resell at churches. That was a tremendous help in meeting the ongoing costs of the ministry, which were significant. We were booking well over 400 meetings a year, not including the lunchtime school performances, and crisscrossing the length and breadth of the United Kingdom.

Nevertheless, it was the churches themselves who continued to be our main source of income, always on the same policy of 'bless the next church.' The churches we ministered to varied hugely, from tiny parishes to big city congregations, but all were treated equally in our 'living by faith' adventure. It was well known that we would not move a small church's booking to make room for a bigger church, and God rewarded that faithfulness time and time again.

We weren't only visiting Elim churches. The 70's were a time of charismatic renewal, particularly in Baptist and Anglican churches. We weren't everyone's cup of tea, with our matching outfits, sideburns and loud music. Yet pastors convinced their conservative congregations to let us come, generally from a desire to reach out to their communities, and get people to come to church. I remember one little church in particular, which met in an old corrugated iron community hall. The pastor had been at Bible college with us. It was cramped and the floor wasn't straight.

I said quietly to Oliver, "If we turn up the speakers, we're going to blow the back wall out!"

We somehow set up all our gear in the available space, tripping over people's feet, and we hadn't sung a note yet, when the pastor got up to address the congregation in his broad cockney accent.

"Well, then, welcome to our church, like," he began. "You've heard of the Crystal Cathedral, ain'tcha?"

Robert Schuller's Crystal Cathedral in California was well known at the time. He went on.

"This ain't the Crystal Cathedral, innit? This is the shack o' yesteryear!"

The elders looked very unhappy, but the crowd loved it!

"Well, we've got Rufaro here, haven't we then? And they're gonna sing then, ain't they?!"

We sang and preached, and it was a great meeting. There was a real move of God, and then it was time for the Sunday evening offering. The treasurer stood up to give the last week's figures, as was their custom, and then the offering bags were handed round. We could see that people were giving generously, and the treasurer's eyes were growing big as he watched the bags fill.

"Bring the bags, bring 'em up!" said the pastor, and the bulging bags were brought to the front. From the looks on people's faces, this was not the norm for a Sunday night.

"While Rufaro were ministering, the Lord spoke to me, didn't He?" he said, looking out over his congregation. "And He told me what to do, didn't He? So I'm gonna do it, aren't I?"

He scooped up the overflowing bags and wobbled over to me.

"What did the Lord say? He said, 'Give all this money to Rufaro,' so they can go and bless other people, can't they?"

I think the poor old treasurer nearly had a heart attack, but the congregation loved it. That offering was more than four times as much as their usual Sunday offering, and this tiny church had indeed blessed us with enough to get to the next place on our calendar.

Time and again, we saw that God would provide, no matter how insignificant a place might seem in our own eyes. Whether a church was big or small, whether the next place was close or far, there was always enough to meet our obligations, and to feed our families. We truly came to know the truth of Philippians 4:19 (NIV);

"And my God will meet all your needs according to the riches of his glory in Christ Jesus."

A fresh call of God

By 1979, we had established Rufaro well enough that we could make another move, this time to Birmingham. We moved into a bigger house, this one with enough room for us all, including Oliver and Brigitte's first child, Donna. Bookings were still coming in thick and fast, and yes, we were still living by the same faith rule, trusting God for all our needs as we continued to serve Him and follow His call.

Living so far away from our families in Africa was a sacrifice, but even there, God was kind to us, bringing us people who would be family to us. Two of those were the 'Birmingham grannies,' as our children called them, Anne and Sadie, who relished spoiling our little ones and offered a welcome grandmotherly influence in all our lives.

One day, we were over at Granny Anne's house, having a good English cuppa, when she asked if I could help assemble a flat-pack cupboard she'd bought. Naturally, I said yes, and as I busied myself in the bedroom with that, I noticed a magazine lying on the bed. It was printed on flimsy paper, the kind used for airmail in those days. It was titled 'Revival Report' and was from an organization run by Reinhard Bonnke, a name familiar to me. It was lying open to a page that said, "We're building the biggest tent in the world. We need to buy 18-wheeler trucks from Colonel Gaddafi, and we need your help."

"Well, that's interesting," I thought, intrigued, as always, by anything to do with the motor world. As I kept reading, I felt the distinct prompting of the Holy Spirit, saying, "The Lord has a role for you to play in this ministry."

Nah, nonsense, can't be… I carried on building the cupboard, trying to shake that 'cheesy feeling'. But my eyes kept drifting back to the magazine, and I kept feeling that tug. "You have a role to play in this ministry." I didn't want to hear it. By the time I had finished building the cupboard, I knew it wasn't going away, and later that day, I told Vangi.

"Let's not tell Ollie anything yet," my wise wife said. "Let's wait and see." And that was where we left it.

About a month later, a pastor of a big church in Birmingham, whom we knew well, gave me a call.

"Look, I know your policy," he said. "I know you don't move bookings from a small church for a big church, but something has come up. We have an unprecedented opportunity to host a big 5-night Gospel campaign in the Birmingham City Hall. We've got a well-known evangelist, but we want Rufaro to come and lead the music, be the conveners, run the meetings, everything…"

"When?" I asked. He told me. "Oh, no, we have bookings then," I said. It was about five months away.

"I knew you'd say that," said the pastor.

"Who is the evangelist?" I asked.

"A German guy from South Africa, called Reinhard Bonnke."

What?? Surely this was no coincidence!

"Let me work on it," I replied.

I phoned around, and without exception, each church that I explained to was willing to move their dates, and we committed to the campaign.

When the time came, we did our part, and as we were packing up on the final night, I asked Reinhard if I could meet with him briefly where he was staying. It was already past 10 pm when I got there. I told him about the magazine article and what I believed God had said to me. He was a little taken aback.

"I'm sorry, Peter, but we really don't have any use for a preacher or a musician. There's nothing for you."

"Oh," I said, disappointed. "I really felt the Lord spoke to me."

There was an uncomfortable silence. I thought I'd better get going, and stood up to take my leave. But then Reinhard said, "Well there IS one thing. But it's nothing for you."

"What is that?" I asked.

"Well, I need someone to kick our transport department into shape."

"Reinhard, that was my profession! I was the managing director of a motor dealership. I'm a skilled engineer. I know that world!"

"What? Would you come for that?" he asked me, amazed.

"I would."

"I'm on my way to Norway,' Reinhard said. "Let me phone you at the end of the week."

When that phone call came, Reinhard got straight to the point. "Have you changed your mind?"

Quite to the contrary, I felt that I had received two confirmations that I was on the right track. Right then and there, I committed to joining Christ for all Nations. I told Reinhard we would need three months to meet our obligations to Rufaro bookings, to sell our belongings and find the money to move the family.

It seemed crazy to everyone who knew us, certainly to all the pastors and churches that had come to know and love Rufaro.

Why on earth would I consider leaving this thriving ministry, at the height of its success, to go and be a motor mechanic? The executives at Elim pondered whether they could even allow me to maintain my ordination, as they "ordained ministers, not motor mechanics," but after due consideration, they were willing to wait and see for six months.

The ever-insistent voice of the Holy Spirit was speaking to me, and I knew that this was the next step in following the call of God. As Oliver prepared for his own next phase as a solo artist, and as we sold up everything we had, we knew that God would not let us down. Once again, we would be starting from scratch, but we were certain He knew what He was doing. With our children in tow, we said goodbye to England, and made our way once more to African shores, this time to Johannesburg. If fixing trucks was what God wanted me to do, then that's what I would do.

Any questions?

It was a hot sunny day when we arrived in Witfield, Johannesburg, to join Christ for all Nations. All the team were accommodated in a huge compound, with the CfaN offices and a large truck workshop also on site. Our family was allocated the lower floor of the original old farmhouse and Vangi began the work of making us a home from odds and ends and furniture donated by friends of the ministry.

My work lay elsewhere and I set about the job of organizing CfaN's chaotic transport department. Besides the fleet of rugged off-road trucks that would soon be needed to transport the new Big Tent I'd read about in England, there were also numerous ministry vehicles. CfaN itself was staffed with an army of volunteers, carrying out all kinds of different ministries, and everybody had a car in need of repair. No one was really in charge of the day-to-day ministry needs. In fact, it was like the Book of Judges – "…every man did that which was right in his own eyes!" (Judges 17:6 NIV)

The first order of the day was the workshop itself. It was a lovely building, suited for the task, but had clearly never been organized by any kind of engineer. I put on my trusty blue coveralls and tackled the mammoth task of emptying it out. Then Vangi and I got down on our knees and painted every inch of that floor with hard-wearing grey concrete paint. After that, we unearthed a little office from under piles of junk and lost tools, and I started putting in the control systems that would get everything working smoothly.

Before long, vehicles that had been languishing in the workshop were back out on the road, and the transport department was running like the proverbial well-oiled machine it was meant to be. One day, about four months after I had started, I looked up from the engine I was working on to see Reinhard striding purposefully across the lawn that separated the workshop from the office building. I could see from the way he was walking that something serious was going on. As he reached me, he called out:

"Peter! I want you to come with me to Reception right now. I've called all the staff together."

I'd vaguely heard something on the PA system a couple minutes before.

"They're all coming to the office," Reinhard said. "I want you to come."

"Now?"

"Yes, now! I'll tell you about it as we walk."

I set the wrench down, wiped my hands hurriedly and fell into step. It wasn't very far to the office, and Reinhard was talking quickly.

"Peter, I want you to be the General Coordinator."

"The what?"

"The General Coordinator! That's the job Marco used to do. It means running everything."

"Reinhard," I said, shocked, "What about the workshop?"

"Never mind, we'll talk later," he said. We had reached the crowd of CfaN people, waiting expectantly in the Reception area.

"I want to tell you all," Reinhard said, and pointed to me, standing next to him in my blue coveralls. "From today, Peter will be the General Coordinator. That's the job that Marco Schwartz used to do, and now he is the man who is going to do it. And that's his office over there." He waved vaguely at the empty office next to his.

"Any questions?" There was a bewildered silence. "Hallelujah!" he said, and marched swiftly off to his office.

The staff dispersed, and I walked into my new office, bemused. I sat down at the big empty desk with a lonely telephone on it, shuffled in the chair for a moment, still in my blue coveralls, and then I quietly slipped out and made my way back to the workshop. I hadn't been there for an hour before the stream of people began, each one with something that needed to be decided on, organized or done. Within a couple of weeks, I had found a willing and competent mechanic to take over the workshop, and I found myself in the place I filled from then on – right by Reinhard's side.

As it turned out, news of this change in position somehow made its way across the sea, and when the six-month term was up, Elim renewed my ordination, and I hold credentials with them to this day.

CHAPTER 5

- What does the Lord need an engineer for?
- A small-town boy in the Big Apple
- One for the people

What does the Lord need an engineer for?

In the Rufaro years, when we were singing and preaching in England, I said to Vangi a few times, "I wonder why God wasted the first 27 years of my life with all that engineering?" I had an excellent grounding in motor engineering and aviation engineering, and there I was, learning Greek, Hebrew and Hermeneutics. It seemed a bit of a waste. But nothing is wasted in God's economy, and I would soon see exactly why and how the Lord had prepared me for this next phase of His call on my life.

The day that Reinhard had marched over to the workshop, the immediate problem to hand was the building of our Big Tent. We were literally building the tent ourselves, taking on a challenge that was unheard of then and may well still be unequalled anywhere else. On a nearby site, great bales of special fabric, newly invented for us by a well-known American engineering company, were being laboriously cut and glued together.

The engineer in charge, a man of great talent but little understanding of how to work with people, was not coping well. As new as I was to CfaN, it was up to me to jump in, boots and all, pull the team together, and take over. As many as 90 percent of our staff were technical people, and that's a group I understand well. Ruffled feathers were smoothed over, relationships rebuilt, and the work was soon back on track.

This was no small job to be overseeing, since the Big Tent was a record-breaking mobile structure that required innovative approaches for practically everything. When complete, it would seat 34,000 under 17,000 square meters of fabric, 27 meters high – a mighty technical challenge. It finally went up for the first time in Johannesburg, to our immense joy, and was filled to capacity.

Every time a big crowd of people meets for whatever reason, getting an idea of the actual size or number of the crowd is always important and often very controversial. There are many agendas that can influence the publication of this number, usually in the direction of exaggeration. Vested interests on the part of organizers and fundraisers, or simply big egos, often cause reporters and writers to turn a blind eye to reason and to default to obvious exaggerations with statements like, "The police said the crowd was…," or "Local leaders gave the number as …"

As Christ for all Nations began to see bigger and bigger crowds of people attending our meetings, we too came under this pressure regarding reporting the size of our crowds. As it turned out, the responsibility for giving numbers, along with a lot of other event-related information, landed in my lap.

With the Big Tent, the problem was non-existent. The tent had seats, made by our team, and they numbered 34,000. But just a few weeks before the second tent campaign was to take place in Cape Town, the Big Tent was destroyed by a freak storm, and that changed everything. The publicity given to the disaster by the press was huge. They delight themselves in 'bad news' and they had a field day with this juicy tidbit. But the news turned out to be anything BUT bad for the event.

People across the city of Cape Town, who may never have responded to our own publicity, were moved to action, their interest piqued. The result was that when the campaign took place, without the tent covering and just on the seats in the open air, the crowd attending was massive. The seats were quickly filled, and a large crowd stood closely together on the perimeter. They looked to us, at that time, like a sea of people. We were rejoicing, but how could we tell how many were in attendance? The million-dollar question! I could figure out the 34,000 seated attendees, but how on earth could we count the even bigger crowd standing behind them? Then I got some inspiration, I believe, from the Holy Spirit.

The big tent was a technical marvel and required hundreds of ground anchors to be drilled into the earth to secure the great structure. To achieve this accurately, we worked from a very detailed map and plan of the site to locate the anchors and masts correctly. I called for the blueprint of the site and looking at it, I knew right away that we could calculate the exact area that the standing part of the crowd were using.

I did this by physically walking around the crowd with the site plan in hand and drawing the crowd on the paper. We then measured the density of the people standing by counting how many were standing in a square meter. The result was easily obtained by multiplying the area covered by standing people, with the density per square meter. This gave a figure for the standing crowd and when added to the known seated people, we had a total. It was 74,000!

I have used this method of counting for every single CfaN open air meeting from that day to this – and that was in 1986. It is definitely not an exact 'head count,' but when done carefully, I believe it is within 10% of the true count. It has worked well to help us assess the efficiency of our promotion activities, the dimension of our follow-up programs and perhaps most important of all, it has served to bring some degree of sanity into the whole matter of crowd-size reporting.

In the early years of doing this, I was often confronted by people holding a photo of some other organization's crowd alongside one of CfaN's crowd photos, while asking the question, "They say their crowd is one million and you report your photo as three hundred thousand, but your crowd is clearly much bigger. How is this possible?"

I never commented on anyone else's crowd count, but simply said, "I don't know how they count their crowd, but this is what we do." And I would outline our counting method. Over the years, it was evident that others began to be more careful with their published numbers too, and I believe that this is not only righteous but also God-honoring.

A small-town boy in the Big Apple

While the destruction of the tent had no adverse effect on the ministry, and probably even brought more souls into the Kingdom, there was still the issue of our broken tent to be dealt with. It was up to me – by now the General Manager as well as the guy with the technical insight – to fly to New York and meet with the engineering company who had made the fabric. We felt that they were responsible for the fact that our multi-million-dollar tent had blown away in pieces. I duly arrived in New York, suitcase in tow, and when I entered the room where six engineers were waiting, I thought, "Oh Lord, I am way out of my depth here!" It seemed best to keep a low profile, listen and pay attention.

One by one, these very knowledgeable men held court, throwing in plenty of diagrams and charts for good measure. They came up with one reason after another why their fabric was not at fault, and why it was this or that reason instead. Then the top design engineer stood up for his turn, and as he spoke, a few things he said got my attention. They just didn't make sense to my basic technical mind. I made a note, and the gentleman continued to talk, building all his arguments on that faulty premise. After he'd been at it for a good forty minutes or so, I raised my hand.

"Could I just say something?" I asked, "It's more of a question, really." The executive chairing the meeting nodded and said, "Sure! What is it?"

"Well," I said, "The gentleman who's just been talking said right at the beginning that …" and I explained what he'd said that wasn't right. "And that's just not possible," I continued, and elaborated as to how his original faulty premise had given rise to an equally faulty argument.

There was an awkward silence around the table. People looked at each other. I waited to be shot down and kicked out of the room or at least put firmly back in my place. The chairman cleared his throat. "It's nearly lunch, "he said, "Why don't we take a recess?"

Off I went with a couple of the guys to go and find out if New York pizza was all it was cracked up to be. After an hour, we were back in the boardroom. To my surprise, everything had changed, as the argument had indeed been completely wrong. After the same thing had happened another three times, me noting basic engineering mistakes that derailed their reasoning and excuses for the fabric failure, I could see the chairman's face blanching when I put up my hand to comment. He ended the meeting saying, "Well, I think we've done enough of this now. We need to go back and look at the recovery process."

In time, they engineered completely new fabric for us, better and stronger, and at a very good price, helping to carry at least some of the costs we had incurred. After all that, I said to Vangi, "Now I understand what the Lord was doing all along, training me in engineering, running a business, working with technical teams, then preaching and singing and teaching. Here at CfaN, I'm using all of it!"

That's the way of it when you follow the call of God on your life. He uses everything we have, and surprises us with what He finds useful as He uses us to build the Kingdom. So often, we think it's only preaching and evangelism that God needs, but He has a place for each one of us. He knows us completely, and you'll find your passions and interests woven into God's plans for your life, in unexpected and deeply satisfying ways.

Before I leave the subject of the Big Tent, let me answer a question many have asked in the years since we built it and rebuilt it – and then promptly outgrew it. As a mission partner asked Reinhard at a fundraising event in Germany many years ago, "What was the point of the Big Tent? All the years of putting it together, raising funds, all the hype? And then it blew away?"

A brother standing by jumped in to answer. "Reinhard," he said, "I think your big tent was the most expensive advertising campaign in the history of Christendom!"

Reinhard replied immediately. "No, it was not an expensive advertising campaign. I'll tell you what it was. The Big Tent was the rocket ship that launched us. And a rocket ship that launches a satellite into orbit is huge, and the satellite is small. It rises into the sky to tremendous heights and then the rocket stops, falls back to earth and is finished. But the satellite is in orbit. And that's exactly what the Big Tent has done. It has launched us into orbit. And from now on, we don't need the tent. The Lord told us, 'My glory will be your canopy, and my praises will be the masts that hold the canopy up.'"

The Big Tent was used just one more time after Cape Town, in Harare. But for the very next campaign after that, in Malawi, we knew we couldn't pitch it. The buzz in the area was enormous, and we knew there would be too many people. Sure enough, the crowd on the final night was 150,000, by our count. We've never again had a campaign as 'small' as 34,000! The Big Tent was a launching device for the ministry, and though we use some of its masts and rigging to this day in our open-air meetings, we have long since left the 'rocket ship' behind.

One for the people

During those early years, the Big Tent time, the Christ for all Nations ministry was based in South Africa, where the ministry had begun. The whole team, including our family, lived and worked on a large compound on the East Rand, in a suburb called Witfield. It was part of the politically conservative town of Boksburg. This was during the apartheid period, so 'conservative' meant strongly supportive of that political philosophy. Boksburg was, in fact, the very last town in all South Africa to set aside the 'Group Areas Act'[1] when apartheid was ending.

CfaN, however, had a different outlook and we had black African brothers and sisters living on the site with us. As it turned out, this was not well received by the residents in the neighboring suburb. We learned one day that they had banded together and were taking us to court for a few different reasons, including infractions of the apartheid laws.

---

[1] **Group Areas Act** was the title of three acts that the Parliament of South Africa enacted under the apartheid government of South Africa. The acts assigned racial groups to different residential and business sections in urban areas in a system of urban apartheid. An effect of the law was to exclude non-whites from living in the most developed areas, which were restricted to Whites.

I was advised by some of our board members to get the best Jewish lawyer (the Jewish community were well-known for their 'liberal' anti-apartheid stance) to help us in what lay ahead. I did this, and after some consultations with him and on viewing the charges that were to be brought against us, we prepared for the upcoming court appearance. When I read the charges that we were to answer, I became quite vocal in the lawyer's office, and set about debunking each charge to him in a somewhat enthusiastic manner. Some of the charges were not unexpected, such as us having people of different races living at our premises together, and allowing hundreds more to attend events on the property. Some were ridiculous, like the accusation that, by traveling far and wide in Africa, we were bringing contagious diseases back to the residents in the area. There were also objections to our big campaign trucks driving through the area.

The court date was set, and I was to be the ministry representative.

On the day, we arrived in court at Boksburg and I saw, for the first time, the panel of stern-looking local residents who were there to bring charges against us. I sat next to our clever lawyer and hoped for the best, breathing a silent prayer.

The prosecutor outlined the charges and added his points, all in a droning monotone that would have put a chronic insomniac to sleep. When he was done, the judge addressed our lawyer and said he should respond. I was surprised when the lawyer asked the judge for a two-minute recess while he talked with his client. He then turned to me and in a conspiratorial whisper said, "You must speak now against these charges." I didn't like the idea, but he assured me that he would be ready to jump in and assist me if I needed it and he was so insistent that I agreed.

I rose to my feet and began to give the same enthusiastic denunciation to the court that I had given to our lawyer the day before. I knew it was going well when the judge's advisers, sitting on either side of him, looked up for the first time in the proceedings and gave me their full attention. Even the judge looked interested in this most uncourtly enthusiasm in his courtroom. When I was done, I sat down. Our lawyer leaned across and said that it was excellent. I immediately asked him, tongue in cheek, what we were paying *him* for!

In response to my speech, the judge immediately put the court into recess and with the drop of his gavel, announced that the court would reconvene in forty-five minutes in the carpark of the Christ for all Nations compound. I was stunned. I didn't know for sure where our black staff members were, and I feared for their safety. Being caught living in a 'white area' could easily have resulted in them being arrested and detained, heavily fined and forcibly moved elsewhere. I rushed back to CfaN and announced to all that the court was going to convene there in a matter of minutes. I asked where our African brothers were and was told that they were out shopping, safely away from the premises. I set someone at the front gate to tell them to go back to shopping if the court was still there.

The whole court arrived and set up a table and chairs for the judge and his entourage. His gavel came down again with the words, "This court is now in session!"

And so it was, in our carpark in front of the office building. Right away, the judge said that, with the court in session, they wanted a tour of the CfaN compound. I must point out that Reinhard Bonnke always required a high standard of excellence and this was evident in the whole place, with well-manicured lawns, white painted curbstones and everything in top condition. The judge, with his entourage in tow, followed me around asking questions, like "Who lives there?" and "Who lives in that house?"

I heard comments from some of the legal people that this place was nicer than their own homes, and I smiled to myself.

Then it was back to the carpark and the gavel came down again with the words, "This court is now in recess and will reconvene in thirty minutes in the courthouse."

Back in the courthouse, the judge consulted with his people and then gave his judgement.

He threw out the charges regarding non-white races residing at our place. Then he discounted the charge of hundreds attending events, because part of our property was registered as a church. He asked the residents how many diseases they had gotten from CfaN staff. When the reply was "none," he threw that charge out, too. Then he said that CfaN should redirect its heavy trucks to the rear entrance of our property and that we should build a three-meter high wall between us and the residents of the area.

I was called upon to rise and receive these instructions from the judge, who asked me if I had any questions or comments on his directives. I thanked him for his deliberations and then said that the truck entrance would be completed in the next three days and the high wall would also be erected soon. I couldn't resist adding that we welcomed the high wall so that we wouldn't have to see our unfriendly neighbors. I'm not sure, but I think I saw a small smile appear on the judge's face before he dismissed the proceedings.

This was not my only brush with the racist apartheid system.

At that time, we had many African pastors working for CfaN in various ministry appointments, and one of the leaders was

Reverend Kenneth Meshoe. He was the leading evangelist after Reinhard, and he travelled with us to all our campaigns inside and outside of South Africa, preaching at many of the meetings. At that time, the apartheid government had constructed areas called Bantustans, where black South Africans supposedly would govern themselves and thereby be removed from the population of South Africa. These states were said to be autonomous and every person allocated to them by tribe could no longer be issued South African documents, but only the documents of their particular 'homeland.'

Although Reverend Kenneth Meshoe was born in the capital city of South Africa, Pretoria, and was the son of a South African policeman, he was allocated to one of these sham states and could only get a passport from that state. In protest of this blatant racism, no country outside of South Africa would recognize these puppet states and therefore would not recognize their travel documents either. This meant that Kenneth could not travel with us to our events outside of South Africa.

I was the one who championed his case and, together with him, took the authorities to task on it. We appeared before the commissioner of the city of Boksburg and I had to make the case for Kenneth. On hearing that this man of God was now unable to fulfil the call of God on his life because of a political and bureaucratic anomaly, and that his work was 100% to preach the Gospel to unsaved people, the commissioner at least agreed to review his case.

We were sent away and many were called to prayer on the matter.

Even though I had the feeling that the politically conservative commissioner was not going to move one bit on this request, we were called back a week later to appear again before him. This time, the commissioner asked the questions, mostly about CfaN as an organization, the work that we did and Kenneth's role in it all. Again, we were sent away.

It was two weeks after this second appearance that we again were summoned, this time for Kenneth to receive his South African passport. We were elated, rejoicing at the victory that had so recently seemed an impossibility, and happy that this part of our work for the Lord could continue.

There was, however, a sting in the tail. When we opened his new passport, we saw that in the section relating to citizenship, the word 'undetermined' had been printed. This was sad from a political point of view, but from that day on, Kenneth travelled freely with the team, bringing thousands to repentance across southern Africa. It was not too many years later that he became, and still is, an honorable member of the Parliament of South Africa. He is still a great servant of the Lord.

CHAPTER 6

Before you call, I will answer

In the mid-80's, Reinhard began to speak more and more often of the need for the Gospel in the rest of Africa, in fulfillment of the vision God had given him – "Africa shall be saved, from Cape Town to Cairo!" So we knew it was time to expand out of South Africa, and he felt the Lord had laid it upon his heart to go to West Africa. We didn't know it at the time, but West Africa is home to the greatest population of African people by far. Even though there are 54 sovereign nations on the continent, a quarter of all African people are Nigerian!

It was decided that we would do a research trip to the region, which was much more challenging than it sounds. It was still the apartheid years in South Africa, and it was impossible to gain entry to most African countries, not only if you were a South African, or lived there, but even if you had a single South African stamp in your passport. There was nothing for it but to apply for brand new passports (I had a Zimbabwean passport then, and Reinhard's was German), and then we would fly north via Zimbabwe. During our stop there, we made sure there was not a single thing in our luggage or papers that could link us to South Africa, and on we went.

Our plan was to go to Cameroon first, from there to Ghana, onward to Nigeria and the Ivory Coast, and then home again via Zimbabwe. We knew absolutely no one in those countries, but we had a few contacts written down, missionaries in each place whom we'd heard of through other ministries. And we had a small kitty of assorted currencies that had accumulated in our office from African believers' postal gifts over the years. With this little package in hand, we hoped to simply meet people once we got to each place, "sniff the air," as Reinhard would say, and figure things out from there.

You might wonder why we didn't just phone ahead. Communications throughout Africa were generally terrible then. While local telephone networks might be in operation, it was close to impossible to get a long-distance call through to any West African country, and telefax had yet to become widespread in the developing world. With a good amount of prayer, the blessings of our co-workers, and dressed in our finest suits, we set off on the first leg of our journey, to Cameroon.

Flights were scarce and flight-paths convoluted, so we had no choice but to get a connecting flight in Zambia, arriving after midnight in Douala, Cameroon. As the plane was coming in to land, Reinhard leaned over and said to me, "Peter, I know a German missionary who used to work in Cameroon. He said Douala is a very dangerous place. We mustn't leave the airport by ourselves, because people get hijacked and murdered for the sake of their luggage, never mind for money."

We disembarked and made our way to customs, where every traveler had to fill in a form, including their occupation. I filled in for both of us the way we always did – 'Minister of Religion.' And then we waited. One by one, all the other passengers left customs, until we were the only ones there. "Attendez, attendez," (wait, wait) the officials said, politely but firmly. No one spoke English, only French. What was the delay? By now, an entire hour had gone by, and every now and then, Reinhard would remind me that we were not to leave the airport without help. Just as we were really starting to worry, another official came up to me, clearly trying to ask me something.

"Ministre? Ministre?" he asked, pointing at the two of us.

"Yes, yes!" I answered. "We're ministers. We're pastors."

"Oh!" He slapped his leg, laughing. "Pasteur! Pasteur!"

They had thought we were government ministers, Ministers of Religion! We certainly looked the part in our best suits. Now that this misunderstanding had been cleared up, we were bustled along into the customs inspection area. Back then, customs in any African nation meant having your suitcases unpacked and every bit of luggage scrutinized. Right next to the inspectors was a huge glass wall to the outside where many people stood with their noses literally pressed to the glass, watching every item in our cases with great interest. It was deeply uncomfortable to be stared at like that, and it only made us more certain that leaving the airport alone would be a very bad idea indeed.

As soon as we were in the main arrivals hall, almost completely deserted by this late hour, I told Reinhard I'd try to call the local Assemblies of God missionary whose number I had. I rifled through the kitty and found a single Cameroonian banknote, which I hoped would be enough for a call. And then I went looking for a pay phone, leaving Reinhard to guard our suitcases.

Over on one side was a bank of phones, but they all took coins. I looked around for someone to help me, and seeing a man close by, I asked him if he could give me change for the banknote and handed it to him. The poor man went ashen with fear, pushed it back hurriedly into my hand, and in an urgent whisper said, "Bad money! Where you get this money from? Hide it! Put it away!"

I did as I was told, hoping I wasn't noticed as I stuffed the note in my sock. He made it clear in a mixture of broken French and English that this was old currency with a former president's face on it, repeating, "Bad man! Bad man!" Not only was it no longer valid currency, but it could also get you a prison stay.

What were we to do now? It was imperative that we get hold of the missionary. There were still crowds of people outside, looking more and more like sharks to me, just waiting for us to leave the secure confines of the terminal.

I was still standing at the pay phones. And then I noticed that, right on the end, one booth was much more modern than the rest. When I looked closer, I could see it was a card phone. That was great, but how was I to get a phone card? Everything in the terminal was closed. The only person in sight was an old man in a dustcoat, cleaning the floor some distance away. With no other options, I headed over to ask for help. To my relief, he spoke English, and said immediately, "Do you want to make a phone call?"

"Yes, I do!" I said, "But I don't have coins."

"I can help you," he said. "I have a phone card." And he pulled out something that looked like a credit card.

"Will you pay me back?" he asked, and I nodded eagerly and said, "Yes!"

He put the card in the phone, and I pulled out the piece of paper with the missionary's number. To my great relief, I got through immediately, even though it was already past 2 o'clock in the morning.

"Hi there," I said to the missionary. "You don't know us personally, but I'm here with Evangelist Reinhard Bonnke, and we're traveling through. We were given your number. We're at Douala airport, we just landed, and we were wondering if we could stay the night with you and make further arrangements in the morning?"

"You're at Douala now?" he said. "I'm right across the city from you. It's going to take me an hour to get to you. But listen! Do NOT leave the airport! Don't go out, no matter what. If they want to chuck you out, don't leave! Just stay put! It's far too dangerous."

Before ringing off, I remembered to ask him how many US dollars would be fair for the phone call. I put the phone back on the hook, and turned around, but the helpful janitor had gone. I assumed he must be sweeping elsewhere, so I took a good walk around the deserted terminal, calling "Hello!" every now and then. But I couldn't find him. Feeling bad that I couldn't repay him as promised, I had no choice but to rejoin Reinhard to wait for the missionary.

Reinhard was glad to see me. I told him I'd made contact, and that the missionary had also said, "Don't leave!"

"I knew it!" said Reinhard, and even when one of the officials tried to make us go, we refused and stood our ground. Eventually, the missionary arrived, and as we squeezed our suitcases into his tiny little car, he said, "It's a good thing you stayed inside the airport. People have been killed here, their bodies never found. It's very dangerous."

As we drove, I told him the story of the 'bad' money, and he laughed.

"That's crazy," he said. "So where did you get the money from to call me?"

"There was a man there who let me use his card. That's why I asked you the amount to pay him back," I explained.

"Oh right!" He nodded. Then looked puzzled. "Wait a minute. A card? You used a card?"

"Yes! At that nice modern little phone on the end, the one that takes cards."

He stayed quiet for a moment, and then with a frown, he said, "Those phones don't work."

"No, no, it worked perfectly!" I said. "I used the card phone and got through to you first time. Excellent service!"

"No," said the missionary firmly, shaking his head. "Those phones do not work. They're a big joke, installed by a French company who didn't even check that they could be linked to our local system. They don't work. They've never worked. And there are no cards for phones here."

I started to protest, but seeing Reinhard looking at me rather oddly, and not wanting to upset our host further, I swallowed my words.

That night, for the first and only time, Reinhard and I shared a bed. "Reinhard," I said, "you sleep under the sheet and I'll sleep on top of it, because I hate hairy legs!" But a laugh and a little discomfort aside, we were deeply grateful to have a welcoming and safe place to stay the night.

Two days later, it was time to leave Cameroon. I hadn't said anything more about the phone, but as I told Reinhard when we got there, there was something I needed to do for the sake of my own sanity. This time, when we arrived at the airport, it was early evening, and the hall was full of people. I approached someone official-looking.

"Excuse me," I said, "I just need to get to the Arrivals hall and check something I saw there when I arrived." Although it was far away, he led me there, and sure enough, I could immediately see the long line of coin phones, with the curvy, modern little booth at the end of the row, on its own pole. I walked straight over to it and lifted the handset. It was dead.

The official who had walked me there was waving his hands and shaking his head.

"No work! No work!" he said, and tried to explain in his limited English that these stupid phones from France had never worked. As he gesticulated and tried to get me to use the coin phones, I ducked around the back of the booth. There were the phone wires, all tied together in a big knot, just hanging out the back of the phone but not connected to anything. I felt like I was going nuts.

Back in the departure hall, Reinhard was waiting. "Did you find the phone?" he asked.

"Reinhard, I found the phone. That phone has never been connected. There are cables hanging out the back, and the guy who took me there said it's all a big joke, and there have never been cards for those phones in this country. But I'm telling you, that old man put his card in that phone, and I phoned the missionary on it. I feel like I'm going crazy!"

Reinhard looked at me for a moment, then smiled and said, "Peter, that man in the dustcoat was an angel."

That stopped me dead in my tracks, and I felt myself nodding slowly. Until that moment, I could not have said for sure that I believed in angels, or at least in that kind of angelic visitation. But our lives were in danger, we were miraculously helped in an impossible situation, and I have no other explanation to give but that God sent an angel to us that night in Douala – an angel in a dustcoat.

A gift of tongues

The research trip that Reinhard and I did through West Africa ended in the francophone country of Ivory Coast. We successfully met with some of the national church leaders and set up contacts for later events, as we had managed to do in the other four places we visited. As we had been staying wherever we could find accommodation, sometimes very rustic, Reinhard announced that for the final two days of our trip, we would book into the best hotel.

The city of Abidjan in Ivory Coast was renowned for some excellent hotels, frequented by tourists from France – and we booked into the best one. It was superb and in stark contrast to the many places we had stayed in on our missionary budget.

For the first evening meal, we decided to give ourselves a treat and went to the famous French restaurant at the very top of the building. It was French cuisine at its best. The plates were huge and the portions were small, but served with exquisite formality and style. Large silver domes were lifted with perfect timing from each plate by attentive waiters, while fresh napkins were tucked into our collars by the head waiter. After each course, our plates were whisked away and it seemed like an eternity before the next huge platter would appear from below the silver dome to reveal more culinary delights. Course after course came and went until the main course was laid before us with a flourish. It was very good indeed and to say that we were delighted would be an understatement.

Toward the end of the excellent main course, the chef came out of the kitchen and appeared at our table. He nodded and smiled, saying something in French that was lost on us. We nodded and smiled back, but he just kept standing there in his full chef's uniform, complete with tall white hat. Every time we looked at him, he nodded and smiled warmly and we did the same - but he remained firmly planted where he was.

As this approached the point of embarrassment, Reinhard whispered that the chef was most probably waiting for a comment on his food. Unfortunately, our total lack of French made this an impossibility and it looked like the chef would not leave until we had said something. The awkward silence grew.

Then I remembered a TV commercial from the days of my youth in English-speaking Zimbabwe. It was an advertisement for tinned green peas, which were being hugely enjoyed by a French-looking person, who after each spoonful would loudly proclaim a compliment in French. I remembered the phrase and turning toward the waiting chef, I touched my fingers to my mouth in the same way that the person in the commercial had done, and with an exaggerated flourish, I announced to the chef, "Formidable! Voilá!"

It worked! The chef burst into a huge smile, and nodding his head vigorously in response, he turned and marched back to his kitchen. Reinhard stared at me in amazement and waited for an explanation of where my sudden French skills had come from. But I just smiled and finished my meal.

Moving North

The vision for Christ for all Nations has always been to preach the gospel 'from Cape Town to Cairo,' so it was inevitable that the ministry would leave South Africa and head north. It was during this time that we wrestled with the question of relocating the CfaN head office. Should it be to Nairobi in

Kenya and then later to Frankfurt, Germany? Or should we go directly to Frankfurt?

During this time, Reinhard once again heard from the Holy Spirit one night. In the dream he was standing at the edge of a deep ditch and needed to get across. While he contemplated how to do this, he heard a voice say to him,

"You cannot cross a ditch in two jumps. It needs one big jump."

On hearing this, we knew what to do. It was to be 'one big jump' for the head office, from Johannesburg to Frankfurt, Germany. Although some argued that this looked as though we were leaving Africa, time proved that in many important ways, we had to leave Africa to reach it with the Gospel.

Even though Christ for all Nations is incorporated in 10 countries around the world, in 2000 the CfaN USA office in Orlando, Florida, became the head office of the ministry. With the faithful and prayerful support of so many wonderful partners in America, this was to be a great factor in the huge harvest of salvations that CfaN has experienced since that time, with literally millions of people being saved – in fact, over 77 million at time of print.

Who could possibly have imagined that our first small steps in obedience to the call of God, so many years before, would take us on a breathtaking life journey across continents, across oceans, and around the world?

Christmas in a container

At every Gospel campaign, we have a team of very capable technicians handling all the highly technical aspects of staging a large open-air event. Derek Murray has headed up this team for decades, directing the acquisition and operation of the huge and complex sound systems that are required for big meetings. Winfried Wentland has directed the transportation and erection of the equipment for even longer. Both are assisted by dedicated men from all over the world.

The 'tech team,' as they are affectionately known, is a unique group who often push through apparently insurmountable problems to achieve technical excellence in the most remote and difficult circumstances.

For every campaign, a compound is set up, usually behind the big platform, from where control of the many and complex technical activities takes place. The tech team uses one of the large containers for a control room, repair shop and restaurant. During the event, good English tea is always available, and this part of the container draws all of us in at various times. The preacher can be found there before going on stage, warming his voice up on a hot 'cuppa.' The photographer is in and out and video cameramen, TV personnel and visitors come and go. Hot mugs of tea are ferried to the staff on the field, and the whole operation seems to be run on hot tea while the smell of cooking pizza fills the air.

This 'tech team hospitality' is also extended to all of us each year in one amazing event – the Christmas Dinner.

Each December, an unwritten law demands that all of us add choice dinner items to our baggage for the trip to Africa. Potatoes, veggies and tea come in from the UK. Coffee, chocolates and cookies come in with the German contingent. Turkey and ham arrive with the USA members and everybody contributes their various culinary skills.

On a day near the end of the December event, the cooking begins. Tables are prepared and decorated, and food is cooked. How they manage to produce an amazing Christmas dinner for around 25 people on just one two-plate stove top is a mystery. But they do. We all crowd into the container and squeeze around the festive-looking table as culinary delights appear, seemingly by magic, on our plates. Party hats are donned, jokes are shared, and we enjoy what must be one of the most unusual and amazing Christmas dinners on the planet.

Most years, the tech team, in their own tongue-in-cheek style, present 'awards' to unsuspecting recipients – awards like 'The Worst Driver of the Year', for some long-forgotten minor infringement, 'The Golden Boot Award' to someone who always puts his foot in his mouth, or even 'The Best-Dressed Man Award' for one technician who allegedly always looked like an unmade bed. These awards, crafted to best represent the failings of the recipients, are presented with great fanfare and received with loud cheers, appropriate heckling and raucous laughter.

When the dinner is over, the team sets to cleaning up and before long the container is back in work mode, ready for the evening meeting and the salvation of tens of thousands.

It's a remarkable group of people, tied together with a common purpose and vision, to see Africa saved, each of us fulfilling our own calling, in the overall vision of Christ for all Nations.

PART 2

Reaching For the Sky

Oh! I have slipped the surly bonds of earth,
And danced the skies on laughter-silvered wings;
Sunward I've climbed, and joined the tumbling mirth
Of sun-split clouds, and done a hundred things
You have not dreamed of – wheeled and soared and
swung.

John Gillespie Magee, Jr.

CHAPTER 7

Learning to fly

A nyone who knows me for longer than five minutes knows that I love to fly. Flying one thing or another has been the abiding personal passion of my life, a pastime that makes me feel that I am directly in contact with God and with the beautiful world He has made for us. It's a passion that has made its way into my ministry in numerous ways. What better way to talk about the leap of faith than with the example of that very real moment of jumping into the unknown from the edge of a cliff? The Holy Spirit knows us each intimately, and He has used my love of flying and adventure to reach into my heart and unlock fresh understanding of what it means to follow His call and to live 'life more abundantly'.

The very first time I ever took to the air under my own control was in a hang glider. It was 1979, and this sport was like a fledgling chick rushing to the edge of the nest to take flight. People all around the world had followed the lead of Australian and Californian 'air hippies' and the colorful delta-shaped gliders could be seen on many a hillside with a 'wannabe' pilot attached and running for all he was worth. My erstwhile fishing partner-in-crime, Anthony Kelton, had the bright idea that we should take up skydiving. Responding to my childhood desire to get airborne, I followed like a lamb led to the slaughter.

As fate would have it, I had been reading with interest about this new aerial activity called hang gliding. When Anthony and I arrived at a small English airfield to sacrifice ourselves to the great skydiving god, my attention was grabbed by a huge advert for 'Hang Gliding Lessons' and the intriguing subtitle that announced, 'The pure way to fly!' I used all my persuasive powers to divert Anthony to the 'pure flight' method and in short order we were signed up for a basic course in hang gliding with the South Wales Hang Gliding Centre.

The five-day course began with technical and aerodynamic theory as well as a first look at this new-fangled contraption. We learned how to assemble and disassemble it and then we learned how to run. In those days, there were no tandem training flights or simulators; just running, running and more running. After three whole days of carrying the glider up a small slope and then running down again, we were doubting that our feet would ever leave the ground and Anthony and I were not averse to letting the instructor know that we felt we were being denied our rights as airmen of the future. His patient and knowing smile told it all.

On the fourth day, the announcement was made that today the weather was good for our first 'high solo' flights. Any thoughts of the risks involved were swept aside by waves of exuberance and pent up anticipation. This was going to be it. After today, I would no longer be a 'flight virgin.' Our group of students arrived at the top of a 200-foot hill and after a few seconds of patient attention grudgingly given to hear our instructor's words of wisdom, we fell upon the gliders and began to assemble them. I remember how I felt as I gazed out over the Welsh valleys and rolling green hills dotted with frosted specks of sheep. The air smelled clean and fresh and the puffy white clouds drifting by seemed as light and buoyant as my spirits. This was air for flying; even a novice could sense that.

But enough of daydreaming. The glider was ready and a first candidate was sought. In typical group mentality, no one wanted to actually be first, despite the verbal bravado of the past hour. Deep and earnest examination of the local flora seemed to engross all of the students simultaneously. The instructor brought the impasse to an end by calling out my name. Why he chose me, I will never know, but maybe it had something to do with me possessing the loudest voice. This had been a source of trouble for me throughout my school and college years and apparently, I had still not got it right.

I put on a brave face and seized the initiative by walking forward. I strapped on the training harness and clipped into the glider while the whole apparatus was carried by many eager hands to within about 10 feet of the edge, facing directly into wind. I could very clearly remember our loud protestations of only an hour ago at the news that we would fly off a 'miserable little 200-foot hill,' but now that this miserable little 200-foot drop was right in front of me, it took on a new and terrifying perspective.

The instructor held the nose of the glider, standing directly in front of me, while confident and smiling students held the wings on either side. For a fleeting moment, I seriously considered the option of feigning a stomach cramp and thereby relinquishing my 'privilege' of first flight to some more worthy recipient, but I steeled myself with the unspoken words that '*this is what it is all about.*' The instructor, who now had my undivided attention, told me to fly straight out from the hill for about 200 yards and then to execute a gentle left turn and land in the field below. He pointed out a small clump of the notorious thorny gorse bushes right in the middle of the chosen landing field, and said that landing in that would 'reap its own rewards.' I made a mental note not to go anywhere near the small patch and thought to myself that I would surely never ever get that far anyway.

The 'sky god,' the favored nickname for instructors, declared that the conditions were perfect and asked me if I was ready and feeling OK. Despite my chosen calling as a man of the cloth, I blatantly lied that I felt great. I did breathe a silent prayer at that moment, asking the Lord above to give me a safe flight. But then I repealed the prayer, not wanting the Almighty to fly this glider. After all, I wanted to fly it, and so I changed the petition to one that I still offer up before every glider launch, even to this day nearly 40 years later. I quietly asked in an unspoken but real communication, for the Lord to *give me a clear head and to help me remember all that I had learned.* I reasoned that this way I would do the flying, which I wanted to do, and still have the faculty of clear thinking and good recall.

All of this took only a few seconds, time being compressed by vast quantities of adrenaline now surging through my veins. Just as I thought it was all going to happen, one of the smug and smiling, overconfident, lucky students holding the wing tip, called out to the instructor with a question. Well, if there was a question to be answered at this late stage, then I, above all others, needed to hear the answer. The smug smiler pointed out that he had noticed that there was only about ten feet of level ground between me and the edge of the hill and he wondered what would happen if the glider was not flying by the time the running pilot reached the edge? I looked at the small distance which separated me and the glider from what was rapidly appearing to be my appointment with doom and felt that the question had a certain validity. I waited with bated breath for great words of comfort and wisdom, but all the instructor said was, "It had better be flying when he gets there!"

He looked at me and in a split second, my entire future and destiny, my aspirations and hopes, hung on one word; "Run!"

I ran. And as I did, I felt the glider being transformed from a lifeless construction of aluminum tubing and Dacron fabric into a living moving creature that began to tug with energy at my harness straps. In the few seconds that it took me to run the few yards to the edge, I experienced that miraculous change of relationship between craft and pilot that happens with every hang glider launch or aircraft takeoff. On the ground, the pilot is the living part of the equation, handling lifeless and inanimate machinery, but when the flow of air touches a wing, the craft springs into a life of its own; living, breathing, moving and reacting. My glider had come alive, and I felt the insistent pull on my harness win the battle over gravity as it lifted me into the air and the ground fell away below.

I was airborne. It worked! The glider and I flew together for a moment and then I paid attention to the required left turn. It was less than perfect but despite my crude and fumbling inputs, the glider did its part and together we changed direction. I could feel its life. I could sense its wants and its quirks. We were flying together.

And now, after what seemed like an eternity in the air, it was time to return to the earth. I concentrated on what I had learned about landing, and all was going well until about ten feet from the ground, I saw to my utter disbelief that I was heading straight for the cursed gorse bush. With great skill and dexterity not often seen in one so inexperienced, I hit it dead center! This piece of aeronautical precision produced howls of laughter and jeers of derision from the crowd at the top of the hill. Did I feel the thorns? Was I offended by their laughter? Not a bit of it. I had flown! I had done it. I was now one of the 'special few' who over the last century have been able to transform their dream of flight into reality. I had overcome all the doubts and fears and survived. I was a pilot, a member of that exclusive brotherhood of people who have touched the edge of the impossible and felt the pulse of the divine. What impact could mere thorns and laughter have on a moment like this?

As I began to dismantle the glider, I couldn't help but think that this first high flight was so similar in many respects to a 'leap of faith,' of which by this time we had made many. There was the extended time of learning why and how a hang glider could carry you through the air. There were instructions on how to do it correctly with examples from others who had already done it. And best of all, we had been witnesses to others flying free above our heads, soaring and diving through the air.

It had been just the same with our search for the call of God and faith to seize it. We learned the theory in church of how and why it works; we eagerly absorbed the teaching on how to appropriate it and we were witnesses to some around us who seemed to soar above the rest of us in faith. But none of this changed anything until, as with the hang glider, I stood on the brink of the cliff and had to decide to go or to wait a bit longer. When I did run, the 'faith glider' gained a life of its own and carried me for the first of many flights – and it still does.

I couldn't get the glider folded up quickly enough to carry it back up the mercilessly steep path to the launch site for another flight. Like so many before me, I had gone from 'interested' to 'totally hooked' in one 45-second flight, and I'm still hopelessly beyond help. As Leonardo da Vinci said in 1452, "For once you have tasted flight, you will walk the earth with your eyes turned skyward; for there you have been, and there you long to return."

There was still much more to be done but now that I had tasted flight, I pressed on with relentless determination. I watched the qualified pilots soaring in their hang gliders for hours at the sites where we were training, and I think I enjoyed their flights as much as they did. I always quietly said to no one in particular, "I'll be there soon."

After qualifying as a Pilot One, as they were called in the UK back then, I scratched together enough money to begin a love affair with a beauty named 'Super Scorpion' – a simple glider by the standards of what we fly today, but state-of-the art in 1980 and the focus of my affections.

It wasn't long before I graduated to the joys of ridge soaring. This activity involves flying along a ridge which has the wind blowing against it at an angle of about ninety degrees, providing a wide band of constant lift in which a skillful pilot can fly for hours. My first soaring flight was at a well-known coastal area in south Wales called Rhossilli and it was there that for the first time, I felt my soul melt into the hugeness of the ethos as I drifted lazily above the beach, watching constantly changing colors as the setting sun painted an extravagant canvas on the sea, apparently just for my benefit.

A seagull floated with me, both of us oblivious to the great differences that separated us at other times, each giving the other the strange respect and acknowledgement that all aviators seem to offer and receive. When the encroaching darkness eventually demanded my return to earth, I floated silently down to the beach and drifted in on a whisper to land next to the softly murmuring surf. After landing, I just stood there, not daring to move, for fear of breaking the balance of this perfect moment in time.

To know flight is to know life.

Skis for the sky

When it was time for us to leave England so that I could join CfaN, we all went, all six of us; myself, Evangeline, the three children AND the Super Scorpion. The booking of airline tickets for this momentous journey hinged around one fact and one fact alone. Which airline offered the best conditions for the hang glider? British Airways won the day with their claim to offer 'special handling for sports equipment' and we arrived at Heathrow airport with three small children in tow and a short-packed hang glider as part of the baggage. Short-packed is a relative statement when it comes to hang gliders, because even in this diminutive-sounding state, she was still four and a half meters long!

I boldly walked up to the check-in desk while Vangi and kids watched over the glider to make sure nobody tripped over it or rushed off to call the bomb squad. Then, I announced that I was the person who had notified them of my need for 'special handling' for an item of sports equipment.

The smiling airline employee behind the counter acknowledged that this information was indeed in the computer and then asked what kind of sports equipment I had. Half under my breath I said, "A hang glider," then brightly added, "I'll bring it right away."

The poor woman's eyes nearly popped out of her head when I lurched towards her counter with this huge package balanced precariously on my shoulder, mumbling "Excuse me" to the many people whose heads had been 'nudged' by my passing. None of this was helped by my daughter giving loud voice to her admiration by shouting out, "Wow, Daddy, you are strong!"

The check-in assistant vanished quicker than a politician's campaign promise, muttering something about a supervisor. A stern-faced woman with an important-looking badge duly appeared. I smiled sheepishly and volunteered to carry it through to the aircraft for her. She looked at me and then at the packaged glider still balancing on my shoulder, and quite without any emotion, she said, "It would have been better to call it skis."

"Are you referring to these skis of mine here on my shoulder?" I quickly replied. She nodded in the affirmative and asked me if I would be so kind as to carry the 'skis' through to the loading bay. Skis to South Africa! I'm sure that was a new one.

Not dressed for the occasion

It was on my very first soaring flight in South Africa that I met a real thermal. I'd learned about thermals, the great rising columns of warm air that can take a pilot way up into the sky, and I was eager to find out what this kind of flying was like.

After many familiarization flights to adjust to the high-altitude conditions of the South African highveld, I chose a soarable day and headed for Krugersdorp, a well-known ridge soaring site not too far from the big city of Johannesburg. In sunny South Africa at that time of year, shorts and a t-shirt were the order of the day. The Super Scorpion was set up and after the usual information chat with the locals, I was ready to launch. I had never seen a launch site before that was covered in rocks, but this was, after all, Africa. I watched the conditions for a while, then launched into the next thermal cycle and was rewarded with an instant rapid climb, leaving my stomach behind to catch up later.

After tracking up and down the slope a few times, I noticed the local pilots congregating at a point toward the end of the ridge, and I did the only sensible thing; I joined them. It was not long before a boomer of a thermal came through and everyone started to climb in a very impressive manner. My only experience of thermals up to this time had been of the undernourished shameful little puffs of tepid air that are passed off as 'thermals' in England. I was quite prepared in my mind to ride this very powerful one for a minute or two and then to have it gently drop me 'out back' so that I could return to the familiar realms of ridge soaring.

What I didn't know was that this baby was about a mile wide! The result was that instead of being 'dropped nicely out the back,'

I continued to climb and climb and climb. The turbulence seemed to never end, and I kept going up like the oil price at an OPEC meeting. Without making one single turn, usually mandatory for any significant thermal height gain, I reached a height of almost 4,000 feet above the ridge. I wondered to myself what all those clanging noises were coming from my previously whisper-silent glider as it was tossed about in the turbulence. I also vowed to myself that if I ever got back to the ground, I would rush out and buy a reserve parachute. (They were not mandatory in those days and I had never even seen one, much less flown with one.)

The next signal that assaulted my senses was that parts of my body no longer seemed to be with me. I was becoming decidedly numb due to the cold at this high altitude, and it was then that I noticed that the other pilots were wearing heavy clothing. For the first time in my flying experience, I wished to be, not up in the air soaring and swooping with the birds, but back on terra firma with some warm clothes on.

So, this was what thermals were all about. When I was back on the ground, I vowed to be better prepared next time and to take the ride to the top!

Hang waiting with the Holy Spirit

We had not been in South Africa long before I had done the necessary familiarization flights. I was now enjoying various flying sites with the small hang gliding community there. One day, several pilots had met at a site to fly. We'd set up our gliders on the top of a hill and were waiting for thermic conditions to develop enough for a flight. As usual, we were sitting near our rigged and ready gliders, watching the weather and talking to each other. We call this 'hang waiting.'

Most of the pilots waiting were unknown to me, and as is so often the case in 'hang waiting,' we were all getting to know each other. I listened to others and told my own story, in which I mentioned that I'd recently arrived from England where I had been involved in a Gospel music group travelling around the UK and that I'd just joined an evangelistic mission here in South Africa.

On hearing this, a young pilot with a British accent spoke for the first time. He asked about our Gospel group and I told him we were known as Rufaro. He got a strange look on his face and said, "I know you. Your group sang at the church that my parents attend in the city of Leeds in Yorkshire."

I was amazed. We had indeed been there several times. I assumed that he was a Christian, but he said that he'd rejected Christianity and had actually left England to get away from his parents' insistence on him going to church. He had come to work in South Africa because it was 'really far away from all that' and had learned to fly a hang glider since arriving. Uncharacteristically, I was speechless, but not for long.

I said to him, "Do you know that there are very few hang glider pilots who are Christians and only one in the whole of South Africa who is an ordained minister? And I ask you the question: What are the chances of you arriving at this flying site on the very day that I am here and for you to end up talking with me?"

I then told him that I didn't have time to talk much with him because the conditions had just become flyable and I was there, like him, to fly. But I did say that because of the amazing fact of us meeting there, I very much thought that God was trying to tell him something. And if I were him, I would go and find a church and get back to a right standing with the Lord.

That was it. The pilots were already moving with their gliders to the launch area and I was right behind them. The young pilot from England also flew, but as he landed much earlier than I did, we didn't meet up again.

It was about six months later, at another flying site during another 'hang waiting' session, that I heard the news that a new pilot who came out from England had just been killed in a flying accident. I asked what his name was – and I was shocked when I heard it. It was the young backslider that I had talked to. My mind whirled with regretful 'what-if's.' What if I had spoken much more to him about Jesus? What if that was the last chance that he had to hear the Gospel again? I was filled with remorse, feeling that I had just not done enough and only because I just wanted to fly. I told Evangeline when I got home, and together we somehow worked around the perceived failure and got on with life.

One year later, I received a letter from England, from the parents of the young hang glider pilot who had been killed in the accident. They said their son had gone to South Africa to get away from being a Christian and not long after he arrived there, he was tragically killed in a hang gliding accident. They had flown to South Africa for his funeral and then returned with heavy hearts to the UK. On arrival back home, they found a letter in the mail from him. They and the letter had passed each other on opposite journeys to and from South Africa. They informed me that in his letter, written not long before the tragic accident, he told them that he had met Peter Vandenberg from Rufaro while on a hillside waiting to fly. He said that Peter told him this meeting was more than a coincidence, that God was trying to tell him something and that he should go and find a church and get back to God. He told them that he did exactly that and recommitted his life to Jesus in an Assemblies of God church, and sometimes even played his guitar in the church music group.

The parents said that they had tried for many months to inform me, but they thought that we were still in England. They finally managed to get a South African address for us and sent the letter. As you can imagine, this news brought a lump to my throat and grateful tears to my eyes. I realized again that the Lord only needs obedience from us, in even the briefest of moments. Then the Holy Spirit is released to do his powerful work.

Hang 'em high

One of our many moves with Christ for all Nations took us to California for a few years. It also turned out to be a remarkable time for aviation. Arriving in the California city of Sacramento, in the center of the San Joaquin valley, I was delighted to find out there were many excellent and even famous hang gliding sites in the region. A close friend of mine, Greg Pearce, who had started learning to fly hang gliders in the UK and who came with us to California, completed his training at a flying school near the city. Being in the middle of a very flat valley, the flying school made extensive use of a launch system known as 'platform towing.'

It was my introduction to towing for hang gliders, and as Greg learned the elementary stuff, I enjoyed many flights from the tow rig. A proficient pilot and tow crew can easily tow a glider to as much as 3,000 feet above the ground. The valley is famous for its stable air, or absence of thermals. This makes it an ideal place for students to learn and I also had many wonderful flights into the late evening, floating about lazily in the silky-smooth air, working every tiny puff of warm rising air to stay up, and then watching the sun set slowly in the west.

It was not long until Greg had completed his initial training and we were free to head for the mighty Sierra Nevada mountains just two hours away by road. The magnitude of these mountain ranges is incredible as they stretch from north to south for hundreds of miles, rising thousands of feet from the valley floor. A favorite flying area for us was near Carson City in Nevada, where many flying sites could be reached in a radius of about thirty miles.

Our first flight from one of these mountains was in the early spring at a site known as McClellan. The launch area is at 7,000 feet above sea level with the valley floor below lying at 5,000 feet. I had, up to then, never seen a launch site that was so rocky and inhospitable-looking, but this was not 'dear old England' with its green grass and sheep. We were right in the heart of the legendary Wild West, and as the stories portray, it is a hard, unforgiving land that doesn't treat the fainthearted kindly. Looking out from the launch site and seeing the snow-capped mountains across the valley, the wide reach of the lake 2,000 feet below and the rugged brown canyons, I had a feeling of identification that I had not experienced since leaving Africa. The place was both inviting and challenging, inspiring and intimidating, a place to get to know but never to become familiar with.

I launched first on that day, right into a thermal cycle that tossed and shook me about for the first few minutes as I turned the glider to fly along the ridge face in search of lift. I had to drag my attention away from the canyons below which looked as though no human foot had ever walked their rugged loneliness. First, I had to fly, and if I didn't pay attention at this early stage of the flight, the possibility of inspecting those canyons 'up close' was more than a remote one. The landing zone was two miles away and I still needed more height to squander on the delights of observation.

Height soon came as thermal after thermal popped me higher and higher. I quickly experienced what, for me, is still one of the true wonders of aviation – the ability to gain altitude in an aircraft without the benefit of petrol and pistons, or gasoline and gears. The very idea that a human being could use his legs to run off a mountain, become airborne, and then by use of intelligence alone, fly around in rising air and gain altitude, remain airborne for hours at a time, cross miles of distance, and then return to earth again landing on those same legs, still sounds to me like the kind of notion that they burned people at the stake for not so long ago. I have never, even after hundreds of such flights, lost sight of the fact that this activity borders on the miraculous and that the relatively few of us who experience it are privileged above all men.

Not long after this first flight in Nevada, I entered a regional hang gliding competition which, as it turned out, took place at the very same mountain I have just described. Having never entered a competition before, I can only attribute this rash decision to unjustified feelings of competence, brought on by too much exposure to high altitude. It was on the second day of this competition that I experienced a remarkable flight.

On the first day, I was greatly intimidated by the lineup of well-known and even world-class pilots that were in attendance to pit their skills against each other. I kept encouraging myself with the rationale that I knew how to climb in a thermal and I knew how to go cross-country, so what could be so difficult? Ignorance truly is bliss, and I was very happy. The first day task was set as a cross-country race to a fixed goal which was 15 miles over the back of the mountain into the high desert of

Nevada. I crowded into the line of pilots impatiently edging their gliders toward the launch area, and before long I was away and climbing.

When I landed an hour later, I was short of the goal but happy to have at least made some distance and scored some points. Later that evening, as the many pilots checked in their flights and talked about the day's conditions, I was being asked about the hang glider that I flew, a British glider with the name Java emblazoned across the upper surface, when a female pilot of US national team fame interrupted the conversation, saying, "Yes, I saw the name while we flew today."

Everyone laughed, because this obviously meant that she was above me and most of the time, above means better in this sport.

The next day, the competition task was set as a race to goal again but this time to a point 21 miles into the high desert. The competition director stated that because the conditions looked so good that day, if anyone wanted to continue on a cross-country flight after reaching goal, then he would allow it if the pilot's driver was present at goal to assist in identification for timing purposes.

Usually a pilot is required to over-fly the goal line at no more than 500 feet above ground level, after which time he would obviously have to turn and land. I remember thinking that if I could just get to the goal I would be deliriously happy. I looked in awe at the 'sky gods' around me, wondering which one would continue going after we mere mortals had struggled as far as we could.

The conditions were indeed excellent, and I was away and climbing fast from the moment of launch. I climbed in thermals with other pilots and after about half an hour I felt that I had a good chance of making goal. I radioed my buddy Greg in the chase vehicle that he should head for goal, as I was on my way. After saying this, I hoped that some great meteorological force of fate would not have me sinking to the ground in the next five miles because of my impudence.

Well, that didn't happen, and by the time that I was within just five miles of the goal line, I was still at 12,000 feet above sea level and climbing strongly towards cloud base. I realized that I would have to make an impressive dive for the ground to pass over the goal line at 500 feet, and then it dawned on me. I could continue and do an extended cross-country flight! Well, why not? I'd surely get another five miles or so. I radioed Greg again and asked him to rush to the officials at goal to assist in identifying me because I was going to pass over goal at about 12,000 feet and continue with the flight.

I was elated at the chatter on the radio which revealed that I was so high that they could hardly see me, but they did and checked my time in, wishing me bon voyage. Now the fun began because suddenly, with the pressure of competition gone, I realized where I was. Here was little ol' me flying my hang glider across the high desert of Nevada at 12,000 feet and already over thirty miles from where I had started.

With each 360-degree turn in the thermals I was treated to the most magnificent panoramic view of desert, salt pans, mountains and lakes. A unique and exhilarating aspect of flying a hang glider is that the pilot has a totally unobstructed view of the earth below. You literally feel as if you are floating miles above the earth and in my opinion the 'feeling' of flight is greatly enhanced compared to other forms of aviation, in the same way that you experience a greater sense of speed when driving a low-slung go-kart as compared to a regular car.

I spotted some buzzards working a thermal just ahead and rushed to join them, thankful for their unknowing assistance in pointing out the rising air. I turned with them, and a more inquisitive member of their group floated over for a closer look at this lumbering, garishly colored bird that seemed to have caught a man in its talons. We flew round and round together looking at each other and I'm not sure who was more fascinated, him or me. After some minutes of gracing me with his presence in this wonderful way, acknowledging each other in an unspoken but common language, the magnificent bird simply thermaled up and away, leaving me to think about my own aerodynamic inadequacies and the fact that up here, I was the 'bird brain.'

The flight continued until I was jolted out of my euphoria by a radio call from Greg down below, pointing out that I was approaching an area of controlled airspace surrounding the famous navy Top Gun flying school. Not wanting to become involuntary cannon fodder, I spiraled down for a landing at a spot 50 miles from launch and although the glider and my body were back on terra firma, my spirit and soul still soared for hours after.

Hang gliding has taught me many things, including this: So often, the goal that we have in mind is far short of where the Holy Spirit wants to take us. If we allow Him to, He will carry us – so much further – on His great wings.

The cherry on the cake came when we returned to Carson City just in time for a pilot's dinner and word had got out that someone had gone 50 miles. My ego got a much-needed boost when I found out that I had been the only pilot to go beyond goal. It was the perfect ending to a marvelous day when the well-known US team pilot of the day before paid me a great compliment by saying loudly enough for all to hear, "I wasn't able to read 'Java' today!"

CHAPTER 8

13

A new pair of wings

The 'call of the skies' could not be avoided for long when it came to power flying. In 1981, once we had begun to settle in South Africa, the opportunity presented itself for me to add a Private Pilot's License to my flying activities. I leapt at the opportunity and like so many before me, I had to scratch the necessary finances together to start the long training process. The Christ for all Nations base in Johannesburg was not far away from Rand Airport, one of the oldest airports in South Africa but now used mostly for general aviation traffic.

With glowing eyes, I signed up at a training establishment and started the life of a student yet again. The chosen aircraft that would usher me into the joys and discipline of power flying was a Piper Cherokee 140 with the registration of ZS-FMC. 'Fox Mike Charlie' was already a famous lady even in those days and had over 5,000 flying hours on her airframe when I placed my eager sweaty palms on her well-worn controls for the first time. These days, 'Fox Mike Charlie' carries the honor of having trained the most private pilots in South Africa, and I was one of them.

They say that you never forget your first love or the aircraft that you did your first solo in. What I have just written must be proof of that process, hinting at the deep and seemingly never-ending relationship that a pilot can establish with a flying machine. To this day, I can still bring to vivid memory the unique smell of her little cockpit as she sweltered in the African midday sun, waiting patiently for a student like myself to come and bring her to life again for an hour or two.

And live she did.

When a pilot like me peers into the cockpit of a parked aircraft, he doesn't see the starter switch simply as a device for making an engine run. With the awareness that comes from flight, he sees the key to indescribable possibilities, the means by which a man can soar and rise and float, the portal through which he can pass into the delights of a world of flight and be free from the earth and all its restrictions – a world that is shared only by a pilot and his machine.

Every time that I had a one-hour flight lesson scheduled, the build up to it would be reminiscent of a wedding day or a college graduation. My whole being and thought processes would revolve around the coming event – the knowledge that at a fixed time in the future, I would step boldly out to meet the waiting aircraft on the tarmac and my presence in the machine would be the catalyst to make it come alive.

These were not so much days of learning, but more like a courtship, as I got to know the hidden secrets of 'Fox Mike Charlie' and she in turn patiently allowed me to learn the charm and gentle touch of a pilot. As my knowledge of her secrets grew and she became more responsive to my touch, I could feel the beginnings of a 'pilot' rising within me. If 'Fox Mike Charlie' was not fit for flight for any reason, I almost felt disloyal climbing into one of the other aircraft and sharing my 'touch and togetherness' with a complete stranger. After all, 'Fox Mike Charlie' knew me and I knew and understood her too.

Not for me the casual flirting with every new and better craft, behavior that I had seen in corporate pilots with golden stripes all over their arms. None of that snide behind-the-hand talk that 'she was getting old and short of performance' that I heard from some students who seemed to value only the flash of new paint and the smell of leather. Not for me to use her for my ends just

113

to get ahead and fly a bigger and better machine. No, 'Fox Mike Charlie' and I would see it through to the end. And we did.

Flying Deck Chair

During my training, I had become something of an item of interest at the flying school, given that I was a minister of religion and a hang glider pilot. Possibly they had never had either of these varieties as students before and now to find both in one seemed something of a novelty. The school was owned and run by a well-known pilot who was a senior captain flying jumbo jets, and it was obvious to me that all the staff paid him great homage and seemed to live in awe of his every word. Apparently, he had been informed of the new arrival.

One morning, as I was in the front office logging the results of a recently completed flight, the man himself walked in. I knew it was him even before I turned around, because of the instant change in the staff from 'ho hum' to 'he-who-pays-the-salary-is-here' mode. The Captain passed his blessings out to all and sundry and then my instructor, Bill, seized the opportunity to introduce the 'novelty' to the great man. He looked just like any other man to me and we shook hands warmly. Then he prepared himself to speak. I could almost hear the heartbeats of the staff as they waited for the honey of his words to drip from his mouth.

"So, you're a hang glider pilot," he said, rather than asked, and my chest swelled just a little with pride that I was at least not a complete novice in the world of aviation, even if I could sense that he would probably not consider hang gliding as part of that world at all.

"Yes sir," I replied, somehow finding the absolute reverence a bit contagious.

His next statement was the big one.

"How in the world can you fly in one of those things? They look like deck chairs!"

This crushing judgement was greeted by polite smiles and chuckles from the faithful and I couldn't resist the quick repartee that had got me into so much trouble in the past. Without answering his question, I launched into my own response.

"I understand that you fly jumbo jets?" and I'm sure I could see his chest swell as the faithful all nodded silently and knowingly.

In response to his affirmative reply, I sailed forth with the coup de grâce.

"How in the world can you fly in one of those things? They look like apartment blocks!"

There was a collective gasp of horror, and the faithful looked at me as if the earth would open and I'd be swallowed before their very eyes. Every eye then turned to the man, whose face broke out in a broad grin – and then a deep rumble turned into an explosion of laughter. The faithful were completely taken by surprise at this unexpected turn of events and the best they could do was to titter softly behind foolish grins.

The Captain, still huffing and puffing with laughter, took me by the shoulder and ushered me into his office calling back to the spluttering followers for tea and cookies. We became good friends and maybe he eventually saw that hang gliding was a part of his world too.

Fools rush in

I was a very new power pilot with the ink on my new Private Pilot's license not fully dry yet, but despite this, I felt ready for a long international flight to the city of my birth. We were in Johannesburg, South Africa where the CfaN office was located and I wanted to pilot a small rented aircraft to the city of Harare in Zimbabwe on a mission trip.

I rented a four-seater Cherokee 140, similar to the aircraft that I had just recently qualified on, and then set about preparing for the five-hour flight north into Zimbabwe, a distance of over 500 nautical miles.

At that time, Zimbabwe had recently gained its independence and people in the flying community in South Africa were very wary about my idea of flying up there. I heard all sorts of wild rumors about being shot down if you wandered off your flight path, but as I knew the place, I ignored the wild stories.

The first indication I received that this was not a frequent flying route was when I tried to buy the required aviation charts for the journey. I couldn't find one chart of Zimbabwe until an old friend said that he had one which I could borrow. This was good news until I discovered that it was dated 1938, and the entire country was depicted on one small chart. Knowing the place well, I was undeterred by this less-than-ideal navigation document and went ahead with the plan enthusiastically.

My passenger was to be my trusting wife, Evangeline-the-Favorite, but then one of our CfaN colleagues heard about the trip, and as she needed to get to Harare, she asked to join us. Betty Lore from the United States became passenger number two and the date was set.

I planned the flight meticulously, being very aware of the fact that I had never flown internationally before, and I was conscious of the many rules and regulations that must be met for such an endeavor. Advice on exactly what to do was not forthcoming, as no other pilot that I knew had ever made the journey, so in this regard I was on my own. I calculated the fuel range of the little aircraft and determined that we would have to land near the South African border to refuel before taking on the second part of the journey into Zimbabwe. The obvious place for this refueling was the town of Musina, which was near the northern border.

We set off early in the morning from Rand Airport in Johannesburg and had a most enjoyable flight for the first two and a half hours. As we approached the remote airport on what was a very hot summer's day, I could see from the air that the place, shimmering in the hot sun, looked absolutely deserted. My mind went into overdrive. What if the fueling facility was not open? I knew we didn't have enough fuel either to return or to continue, and this could be disastrous. By the time we landed, I was somewhat agitated, because there was not a soul in sight. I was beginning to fear the worst. I saw the fueling station and taxied up to it eagerly, searching for any sign of life – but there was none, just a glaring haze of heat across the tarmac.

In my anxiety, and being new to the role of taxiing an aircraft, I taxied right up to the filling station, completely forgetting that the Cherokee had wings sticking out of each side – and I promptly poked a wing into the side of the little office at the fuel pump. The glass window broke with a crash and I could see the leading edge of the wing crumpling against the steel frame. Vangi cried out, "Reverse, reverse! You're going through the window!" Also new to flying, she didn't know that airplanes have no reverse gear. All I could do was grind to a stop – but too late.

I climbed out to push the plane backwards, and then I saw the ground attendant appear, seemingly out of nowhere, and very angry at the damage to his fueling station. My passengers climbed out as well to huddle under the scant thorn trees, trying to hide from the suffocating heat, while I filled the tanks.

I examined the damaged wing and knew that it needed attention if we were to continue. I needed a plan. After paying for the fuel and the broken window, I got some duct tape from the attendant. Then, finding a rusty shovel and a large stone nearby, I press-ganged Vangi into engineering duty.

"Hold this rock under the wing while I beat the leading edge back into shape," I said, handing her the stone.

She rose valiantly to the occasion, standing on tiptoe to make the best use of all her five foot two inches. With the rock in place, I climbed up on the wing and banged away with the shovel, pieces of rust flying in all directions, desperately trying to restore the wing to a flyable shape. The final touch was the liberal application of duct tape to smooth over the wrinkles.

I can only imagine Betty's thoughts as she sat under a nearby tree, watching this performance with growing discomfort. When it was time to get back on board, she tentatively asked how me much further we had to go. I replied that we were about halfway there, and she looked somewhat alarmed at this news. I assured her that the second part of the journey would be fine, and we climbed aboard for departure.

The takeoff was not altogether normal, given that the wide expanse of tarmac that made up the runway was blisteringly hot in the midday sun and so the air everywhere was very turbulent. The little plane struggled to gain altitude in the extreme heat and we bounced around like a fairground ride. Once at altitude, things became quieter and we settled in for the next two and a half hours to Harare, only to see huge thunderstorms looming across our path ahead. They were mightily impressive, towering around us to 20,000 feet and very obviously beginning to drop tons of water below each one.

I kept as far away as possible from these monsters, weaving in between and passing one after the other. Once again, we were tossed around by strong turbulence. We must have looked like a mosquito in comparison to these behemoths of nature. I became aware of muttering coming from the seat behind me. It was Betty, praying fervently; "We have not inherited a spirit of fear but of a sound mind, we have not inherited a spirit of fear but of a sound mind," which she kept mumbling for a long time, until we had flown away from the storms and the journey settled down again.

I was now working on the estimated time of arrival to give to the air traffic controller in Harare, which I duly did. He asked for our present position and I immediately gave him the name, from my chart, of the small airfield that we were passing over. He asked me to repeat the name, which I did, and then he came back on the air to announce that the name I had given was for an airfield that had been closed fifteen years previously. I guess the chart really was ancient! I then gave him our estimated time of arrival and we cruised on serenely toward Harare, with me pointing out well-known landmarks to Evangeline. Our allocated flight altitude was 10,500 feet, and I was thinking about the timing for our descent to land at Harare, when I drew her attention to a lake I knew was near the city.

It dawned on me, with a sense of horror, that if I could see the lake, we were already over Harare International airport. My estimated time of arrival was way off. I tried to call the airport controller but there was so much international traffic that I couldn't get a word in. My inexperienced pilot mind was being bombarded by radio talk from huge airliners belonging to overseas operators – and here I was in a tiny little single engine plane, flying right into the mix. I couldn't descend without permission, so I just kept on flying right over the top of the airfield, desperately trying to talk to the controller. He had heard me, and very crisply instructed me to stay on course and at the same altitude.

Betty looked down with interest and commented that there was a big airport passing way below us. Which town was that? I didn't reply.

Eventually the controller had time to talk to me, by now way past his airport, and he instructed me to turn around and come back at the same altitude. I did this and as we approached the airfield for the second time, I was desperate to descend and join the landing traffic pattern, but he kept me at altitude. By now, I was perspiring profusely and thinking only that I needed to descend *now*, if I was to land on the numbers at the beginning of the runway, as I had been trained to do. He finally gave me the clearance to descend and I made that little plane come down like a monkey down a tree. This precipitous descent reactivated Betty's backseat intercession.

Down we went, and with great relief, I saw the threshold of the runway approaching. Against all the odds, I had made it to the very beginning of the runway and would land, 'on the numbers.' I looked up and only then realized that the runway at Harare international Airport is about five miles long and here we were – landed, but so far away that we couldn't even see the terminal building.

I started perspiring again as we taxied for what seemed like an eternity at close to flying speed, to get to the terminal before the next passenger jet arrived. My state of mind was not helped at all when, after a while, the controller called on the radio to ask where we were. I simply replied that we were coming!

For some reason, Betty chose to return to South Africa in the passenger seat of a CfaN truck.

Tricks of the trade

I was a student pilot whose training time was often extended, not only due to ignorance or incompetence, for these two are every student's bedfellows, but due to the ever-present pressure of financial lack. This did have one advantage, however, because it gave me many opportunities to fly in the right-hand seat with commercial pilots whom we often contracted in our work to shuttle the team around the country. I saw every opportunity as a God-given gift to learn from the pros, and I gleaned many valuable tips and insights from these great pilots which I applied in my training days.

It was on just such an occasion that we were flying in a Cessna 206, one of the great workhorses of general aviation, and the man in charge was a commercial pilot whom I greatly admired for his skill and professionalism. As always, I was keen to learn from him during this flight. With the CfaN passengers all securely seated in the back, we were on our way to distant parts and he very generously handed the Visual Flight Rules (VFR) chart to me and invited me to do the navigation. As we progressed on our journey with me calling out every recognizable landmark, I noticed thankfully that he was not actually relying on my stuttering hit and miss navigation, but was consulting his ADF and VOR instruments, which are radio beacons.

I continued to do my best, trying to get it all right, and I asked him if professional pilots ever got lost. He admitted that some of them did. I then wanted to know, from an old hand like him, what the remedy was in such a desperate situation. He gave me a few pointers but then added that some guys had got so desperate that, believe it or not, they had flown along a railway line until they found the name of a station that they could then identify on the chart. He laughed at my open-mouthed disbelief and I secretly wondered if he was winding me up.

We droned on for about an hour and a half more, and during this time I could identify less and less of the landmarks on the chart until the scenery below us bore no resemblance to anything on the chart. I kept telling him that I didn't know where we were on this chart and he just kept smiling and looking knowledgeable. After a while, I noticed that he was turning the knobs on the navigation instruments quite a bit more than he had been doing and then, in a serious sounding voice, he asked for the chart. I handed over the useless item to him, despairing that I would ever understand how he knew where we were. Then I saw the look on his face as his head swung from side to side peering down at the scenery below. Hesitantly, I asked him if we were lost. He didn't reply, and we droned on in silence for some time as I watched his now agitated manipulations of every knob on the panel that would turn.

Suddenly, I noticed a railway line coming up ahead on my side of the aircraft and I pointed it out to him as diplomatically as possible, with the weak suggestion that maybe we could find it on the chart. He never spoke or acknowledged my observation, but the Cessna began to bank gently to the right and started a slow descent. The railway line came nearer and nearer until we were flying along parallel to it and in the distance, I could see what appeared to be some small buildings alongside the tracks.

As we got nearer, they were on my side of the aircraft and he leaned over to me and spoke the first words that I had heard from him since the world below us had refused to match the world on the chart.

"See what the name of the station is." His words were quiet but clear.

I announced the sought-after information and immediately, the aircraft turned away and began to climb as he scanned the chart. Within minutes, we were back on course again. Not another word was said about the navigational aberration, or about the 'guys who get so desperate that they fly along a railway line,' but I had learned a valuable lesson.

Don't assume that you know it all, and don't be too proud to ask for directions! This applies to following the call of God, too.

CHAPTER 9

- Taming the beast
- A reluctant assistant
- Out of the jaws of the lion

Taming the beast

Not long after I had kissed 'Fox Mike Charlie' goodbye for the last time, clutching a brand new Private Pilot's License to my chest, CfaN was given a small aircraft to assist us in our work. This completely reinforced my secret belief that God is a pilot! When I saw the machine for the first time, it was love at first sight. She was not a sleek, curvaceous beauty or a broad, motherly transporter of people. She looked more like a 'tomboy' waiting to get involved in some unladylike prank.

She was a Maule M5 taildragger. We are talking 'rag and pipe' stuff here, because although her wings were aluminum covered, her fuselage was made in the time-honored tube and fabric style, reminiscent of an earlier age of aviation. But she was no old bag. I walked around her, taking care not to get too close because she looked like she was ready to pounce. Her extra-large 'tundra' tires made her stance appear even more squat than it was. I heard rumors that under her cowling rested a 210 horsepower, fuel injected, six-cylinder monster of an engine. Witness to this was the huge constant speed propeller proudly cocked at a jaunty angle on her nose. I liked her.

I had 80 hours in my log book, and people wiser than I were giving sage warnings that this machine was not for the fainthearted or inexperienced. The most common description that I heard of her was, "*She can bite you when you least expect it.*" But far from being put off, I was intrigued and fascinated and longed to get to know her for myself. Mr. Maule was famous for the construction of this aircraft and prided himself on her legendary short-field performance.

Others were not so sympathetic and talked long and loud about her notorious vices. Maule's own designation for this model was the 'Lunar Rocket' which tells you something about her lack of subtlety. The first problem I had with her notoriety was when I needed to find an instructor who would be willing to train and convert me to fly her. I met with responses ranging from, "I don't fly Maules," to, "Wouldn't catch me training an 80-hour pilot in one of those!" and many other shorter but unprintable outright refusals accompanied by excessive head shaking.

Just when I was beginning to despair that I would ever find someone capable or foolish enough to take the job on, I met Theo. His casual, "I'll fly anything with wings" was music to my ears but possibly a statement that he would later regret. He was not a subtle pilot and flew her as if she was a wild animal that had to be constantly subdued. I was sure that, despite her reputation, she would respond well to a gentler approach.

This was not to be an easy mutual courtship, as with my first love, 'Fox Mike Charlie,' but something more akin to an arranged marriage complete with sparring mothers-in-law. There was Theo and 'Juliet India Papa', as her registration labelled her, and there was me. On the first flight, he did several takeoffs and landings, perhaps more to familiarize himself than to instruct me, and proceeded to talk about what he had heard of the handling quirks of Maule aircraft in general.

Considering what came out of his mouth, I was amazed that he agreed to teach me to fly her, knowing that in addition to my lack of airtime, I had also never flown a tailwheel aircraft of any type before. We did what we had to do but I think Theo's philosophy on training was pretty much 'I'm here in case anything goes wrong, now get on with it!' What I lacked in knowledge and experience, I sure made up for in enthusiasm, but this man would earn his money.

We taxied to the runway threshold for my first ever takeoff in a Maule and a taildragger. Theo looked as though he had more confidence in me than I had in myself, but I busied myself with all the details knowing that he would help if it all went wrong. As we lined up on the runway, he reminded me about precession, gyroscopic forces, spiraling prop wash and engine torque reaction, all technicalities that are summed up in the fact that EVERYTHING will cause this aircraft to try and turn around and go the opposite way down the runway as soon as you begin your takeoff run.

I advanced the throttle slowly, which I thought important with all that horsepower, and we began to roll slowly forward. The progress must have seemed a little tardy to Theo, because he reached forward and in one cavalier sweep of his hand, he pushed the throttle to the full open position with the comment, "We want to fly, not taxi."

Instantly, every one of the sleeping 210 horses woke up in front with a deafening roar. We lurched forward, and that was the last time I saw the runway. Suddenly, there were now buildings right where the runway had been a moment before and I jammed in as much right rudder as I could. The buildings disappeared as quickly as they'd appeared and were replaced by a vast panorama of huge trees. I hit the left rudder pedal with all my might, thinking to myself, "Where is Theo?" Now the trees were gone but the buildings were back. A fascinating sequence of events set in …. buildings – right rudder – trees – left rudder – buildings again – right rudder – trees again – left rudder, until out of the corner of my adrenalin-enhanced eye, I saw a hand frantically pull the control yoke back and we were airborne.

Theo's comment?

"What's wrong with you? Don't you know how to fly this darn thing?"

I thought to myself, *"No, I don't, that's why I'm paying you,"* but I was too busy to say it. I also thought that I could feel Juliet India Papa chuckling to herself.

Time healed all, as it always does, and I began to realize that she needed a firm and definite hand. When that was given, she became a little pussy cat and all the tiger roar vanished. We were beginning to get to know each other, and I knew I was falling in love again. This was to be the beginning of a long and happy relationship that lasted for many hundreds of airborne hours.

But for now, Theo was still around, and the final hurdle was that I had to be able to demonstrate a wheeler landing. This, for the uninitiated, means landing a tailwheel aircraft on the main wheels only, and as the aircraft slows down, lowering the tailwheel to the ground. Theo set about showing me how it was done. We flew the approach to the runway of a small, almost deserted airport and levelled off just above the touchdown point. He informed me that one needed a little more speed for a wheeler landing and then you just 'squeaked her onto the ground.' He then 'squeaked,' but apparently Juliet India Papa was not in a cooperative mood for we contacted the runway alright and then immediately bounced thirty feet back into the air.

Theo uttered what must have seemed to him to be appropriate expletives, then turned a bright shade of red as he realized who was sitting next to him. As always, the expletives didn't help the situation at all and we had to go around for another try. On the way, he gave me a detailed post-mortem of the recent wheeler attempt and declared that it could just be that he was a little rusty on this particular procedure.

He must have somehow annoyed Juliet India Papa though, because on the next attempt we managed to bounce even higher, although there was a marginal improvement over the first try as far his language was concerned. After five more bounces of varying magnitude and style, punctuated with frequent references to Mr. Maule's ancestry, Theo made an official announcement that it was impossible to do a wheeler in a Maule. I, for one, was relieved because now I wouldn't have to try.

We headed back to the airport with Theo's only comment being that, "This damned thing just converts fuel to noise." I made no comment, quietly smiling to myself and thinking that Juliet India Papa had won the day again and had, in the process, added another chapter to the already substantial urban legend of her family's bad behavior. It would no doubt be retold with vigor for a long time to come.

It was many months later that the seasoned Maule pilot who had donated the aircraft to CfaN, Don Preen, flew with me. Without comment, as if it was the most ordinary daily event, he 'squeaked' her onto the runway in a perfect wheeler landing and I couldn't help but notice his gentle touch on her controls as he caressed her onto the ground. From then on, I became a 'caresser' on every landing, only occasionally relaxing too much and forgetting that deep inside of her there was still a beast hiding.

A reluctant assistant

Don Preen was with us on a campaign one evening, and as we were having a meal together, he related the story of what had happened to him with the previous aircraft he had owned, also a Maule.

He wanted to take a friend for a short pleasure flight but when he tried to start the engine, the battery was flat. The obvious solution was to start the engine by hand-cranking the propeller. This is achieved by having someone sit at the aircraft controls with the brakes firmly applied and the ignition switched on. The throttle is opened slightly and then, when the propeller is pulled forcefully down by hand, the engine should fire and run.

Don said that he did all of this even though his friend was not a pilot, but he told him what to do and the engine started up. However, the throttle was set a little high and the engine started running a bit too fast. His friend at the controls heard this and in his panic to reduce the throttle, he pushed it the wrong way and increased the power. The plane lurched forward, and Don had to dive out of the way to avoid being decapitated by the spinning propeller.

As he lay on the ground, all he could do was watch in horror as the plane accelerated away with the novice at the controls. The plane quickly became airborne and flew in a wide flat circle, just above the ground, until the terrified passenger had the presence of mind to turn the ignition switch off. When the engine died, the plane settled back to the ground and careened into a parked aircraft before coming to a stop. The passenger/pilot was okay, but the plane was damaged.

Reinhard was with us that day as we all listened in amazement to this almost unbelievable story.

Some months later, I was flying Reinhard in our Maule from a remote ranch to a CfaN meeting in a faraway city. We planned to stop at another place on the way where he had an appointment. The flight to the first stopover was uneventful except for one small thing. Unknown to me, the charging circuit on the aircraft alternator had overloaded and tripped, so as we flew, the battery was slowly discharging. When we landed for the short stop, I noticed the problem and rectified it, but the battery was now completely flat and would not crank the engine for our departure.

I informed Reinhard that the only solution was for me to hand crank the prop to start the engine. The little airport was deserted, and Reinhard was the only one available to hold the brakes and handle the controls while I pulled the propeller vigorously for an attempted start. I saw his eyes grow large as his mind went back to the recently-told story about that runaway plane. He looked at me and asked, "Isn't this what Don was doing when his plane took off without him?"

I answered that it was, but with one major difference.

"Reinhard," I said, "the difference is that he had his friend, but I've got you! And you won't make that same mistake."

He climbed into the pilot's seat, and I showed him how to hold the foot brakes on with both feet. I could see the muscles bulging in his legs as he enthusiastically applied maximum power to the two brake pedals. I knew that this Maule was not going anywhere without me.

The engine started, and I ran around the plane to exchange places with Reinhard, whose legs were still powerfully planted on the brake pedals. As we taxied to take off for our final destination, a relieved and smiling Reinhard said to me, "I did better than Don's friend, didn't I?"

My response was, "Reinhard! I never expected anything less from you."

The little Maule and I spent many happy hours in the air, traversing southern Africa, ferrying Reinhard and other staff back and forth to Gospel campaigns in the region. And it was this very same little plane that played the starring role some years later, when a ministry trip to Zambia went terribly wrong, and took us into the jaws of the lion.

Out of the jaws of the lion

In 1986, we were based in Zimbabwe with Christ for all Nations for a nine-month period. During this time, Juliet India Papa acquired a new base for operations, the delightful little airport 'Charles Prince,' outside the city of Harare. It was from here that I flew up to the town of Ndola, in the neighboring country of Zambia, on a flight that became memorable indeed. A German CfaN colleague, Werner Drotleff, and I, headed off in a northerly direction on a three-and-a-half hour flight that would be mostly over open bush, just mile after mile of big game country. The only feature of note on the entire trip would be the international border between Zimbabwe and Zambia, the mighty Zambezi river flowing eastward into Mozambique and the Indian Ocean.

After filing the necessary documents for an international flight, we took off early in the morning. An early flight in the brisk air of an African morning is an experience that washes your soul. So pure is the air and so undisturbed is the atmosphere, you almost feel like an alien intruder in an innocent world. The Maule announced our presence with a full throttle roar as we surged upward through the mists, but I knew that moments after taking flight, she could be soothed back down to a contented purr as we levelled off and headed north across the African plains.

With the sun slowly rising on our right, we transitioned into the wonderful world of being airborne, becoming one with the elements, feeling both elated and reverent, secure and vulnerable.

There is no place for talk at a time like this. My passenger and I silently drank in the awesome spectacle of the day's beginning.

We were on our way.

To fly in Africa in those pre-GPS days was to go back in years to the days of pilotage – the art of navigation by means of chart, compass and timepiece alone. This method in the western world is used almost entirely as a novelty for training pilots and to show them how it used to be done; how Charles Lindbergh did it when he crossed the Atlantic for the first time, and what they would have to do if, heaven forbid, all else failed. Here on this flight of ours, as with so many others, it was a matter of life and death. Yes, we had the instruments, but it seemed that nobody down below ever had the ability to send anything useful to them.

Juliet India Papa was a bush plane, designed for short trips beginning and ending on short and inaccessible rugged runways, and was not really suited to these long international flights. But she took to the challenge with zeal and was faithfully able to cruise through the air at a steady and respectable 120 knots, although 'holding a steady heading' was another matter altogether. Every time a gust of wind or thermal would give her a nudge, that tomboy spirit of hers would respond instantly, and she would tug and pull against my determined resolve to keep her attention on the straight and narrow.

With no autopilot to keep her in line, every minute of every flight was a hands-on affair. I had a small cushion, which I named 'Autopilot,' as I would wedge it under my left elbow on these long flights, to steady my arm and delay the onslaught of muscular collapse. This innovation also allowed me to truthfully refer to 'my autopilot' when in discussion with the kind of pilots who spent their airborne time watching electronic gadgetry flying their aircraft.

Ndola duly appeared under the nose at the anticipated time and we landed and refueled without incident. The plane was left to spend the night alone while we did our business in the town and prepared for the return journey.

After wading through the ever-present bureaucratic shambles the next morning, I optimistically went to the Met office to get a weather forecast for our return route. The not-so-civil servant was at a loss to know why I would want anything more than his local wind speed and direction. It soon became clear that the observation of these two weather features was all he could do. I resigned myself to the fact that I had no option but to get the weather information that I needed in the normal Third World way – when it appeared in the windscreen.

After the usual morning inspection ritual, I coaxed the plane into life. Werner climbed aboard, and before long, we were climbing out in a southerly direction heading for the international border, Zimbabwe and home. Once again, none of the directional aids that pilots usually rely on were operational, so I settled down to the constant vigilance of flying by compass and chart. It was windier than the previous day, but we were soon on the desired track for home. To take advantage of better fuel consumption, I climbed all the way up to 12,500 feet and with Juliet India Papa purring contentedly and the bush country rolling away in all directions for hundreds of miles, we looked forward to a good view of the mighty Zambezi river in about two hours' time.

An experienced old pilot once said to me that the only true constant in aviation is that 'things will change,' and his wise words were soon to come back to interrupt my euphoric flight.

After only a short time, I noticed that a smattering of cloud cover was moving in far below us, but it was well broken up and no problem to our visual flight. As we continued, the balance of options became more pressing as the clouds below seemed to thicken, then disperse again, and thicken once more.

Maintaining this high altitude was serving us well but it was clear that soon we might have to drop below the developing cloud layer to maintain our visual status with the ground, although the higher altitude was more advantageous for radio contact with the now distant controller. Just as the cloud below was looking as though it was time to descend, the Maule gave one of those surprises that keep us pilots on our toes. The directional gyro, vital for maintaining our compass heading, spooled down and stopped working. We had experienced a vacuum pump failure.

There were two options open to us; go back to Ndola or continue the flight using the magnetic compass mounted on the top of the instrument panel. Turbulence shakes the floating compass pointer around making it difficult to read and maintain a heading, but we were in delightfully smooth air at the time and I elected to continue, keeping a watchful eye on the changing cloud density below.

By the time we should have been reaching the border and the mighty Zambezi River, now not easily visible through the broken cloud cover, I was having difficulty raising any of the controllers on the radio. The smooth air had become a thing of the past, with choppy conditions causing the magnetic compass to swerve drunkenly from side to side. After repeatedly failing to raise a response on the radio, I decided it was time to descend and get a better look at the ground below to establish exactly where we were.

Down we went and as we came into clear view of the ground below, I was dumbfounded by what I saw. I had flown extensively in this area, but the mountains and valleys covered in thick jungle that were now below me were totally unfamiliar to me.

It didn't look like Zambia, but it was also not the familiar, relatively open bushveld of Zimbabwe. I checked the charts but found no secrets revealed there. By now, the turbulence that our lower altitude had brought us into was shaking us up and down like a terrier would shake a rat. The compass was swinging about so wildly that it was totally useless and all I could do was try to maintain something of a heading and look for a landing strip in this unfamiliar landscape. I estimated we had about two hours of fuel on board, so I desperately needed to get a fix on our position before this most precious commodity was gone. My stomach churned with an unwelcome realization. We were lost.

It's at a time like this that the very best in every pilot comes out, but you always wonder how you'll respond when that much-feared emergency actually arrives. Now it was happening to me. I surprised myself with my own calm as I assessed the situation and determined not to let Werner and Juliet India Papa down in this most telling of all moments. I would land and find out where we were, then take off again, on course for home.

While scanning the seemingly endless tree-covered mountains for a runway, I managed to contact a commercial airliner passing high overhead above the now-solid cloud cover. I informed them of my predicament and they volunteered various radio beacon frequencies that all proved to be useless at our low altitude. While talking with them on the radio, we flew over a particularly high mountain and in the valley below, a large grass runway miraculously came into view.

I told the airliner that I would land there and ask the way, while remaining on this frequency. I also asked them to inform the controller in Harare about us and our intentions, knowing that as we descended even lower we would most probably lose radio contact with them too. The Captain agreed to do this and wished us luck.

I descended to have a look at the runway. It looked to be in good condition, covered with well-mown grass and with cattle grazing on it, but not a soul in sight. Not even the usual cow herder. I buzzed the runway in a low-level pass to frighten the grazing cattle away, a normal procedure at remote airstrips in Africa, but after three low-level passes, the cattle remained unimpressed and immovable. Nothing moved down there.

We were burning up valuable fuel, so I decided to land in the very short part of the runway that was unoccupied by cattle. We skidded to a halt, a mere 20 feet from the first animal, turned around and taxied back to the threshold to be ready for a quick departure as soon as we had established our whereabouts. I was now more than puzzled by the total absence of humans.

I cut the engine and both Werner and I climbed out. And then we saw them. African children. Scores of African children materialized from the surrounding bush and ran toward us with shouts and squeals of delight. Their courage and volume diminished in direct proportion to the distance remaining between them and us, and they ground to a silent halt about 10 feet away. I smiled at them, and this had the effect of raising their courage and volume simultaneously, and they stormed forward once more. I engaged the first boy to arrive, judging him to be the bravest and probably the cleverest one, asking about our mutual location. I looked directly at him and with the clearest diction possible, I asked,

"Zambia?" He looked blank so I tried another tack. "Zimbabwe?" Still blank.

From the corner of my eye, I could see that Werner, in his own inimitable kids' ministry style, had pulled some party balloons out of his pocket and, much to the delight of the crowd, was blowing them up and handing them out. It was then that I found out where we were.

As one little boy took a balloon from him, he called out in clear and unmistakable tones,

"Muito obrigado!"

That means 'thank you very much' … in Portuguese. To my horror, I realized that we had landed in Mozambique! I did not need anyone to tell me that Mozambique was in the middle of a bitter civil war and that this war was raging in the northwestern region, where we were now parked, dishing out balloons.

Just as this revelation hit me, I looked up to see the bush opening yet again, this time to reveal a group of armed men in tattered military camouflage uniforms, armed to the teeth with guns and bandoliers, walking slowly toward us. I frantically asked Werner what a suitable Portuguese greeting would be and armed with my newly gained knowledge, I pushed through the chattering children. I walked purposefully straight toward the most important looking man in the group, put my hand out for a handshake, and confidently said,

"Bom dia amigo!"

I hoped that it meant good day or something equally positive, and I could see that he was taken aback by this forward approach. He hesitantly took my proffered hand and returned the greeting as I pumped his hand up and down with the vigor of a used-car salesman clinching a deal.

The whole group started smiling and nodding their heads up and down in approval while jabbering at me in Portuguese and gathering round to take their turn at pumping my hand. Still shaking hands, I asked the leader, with words and gestures, which way was Zimbabwe? He consulted one of his comrades in arms and turning to me, pointed authoritatively toward the west and grunted, "Zimbabwe Uh." I made a mental note of the direction and while smiling sweetly at everyone, I called out to Werner in German to get back in the aircraft, as we were about to leave. I was turning to do the same when I heard the 'comrades' remonstrating with each other and saw various members of the group pointing in completely different directions, each grunting, "Zimbabwe Uh!"

I could see that we were not the only ones around here who didn't know where they were, but even though Zimbabwe's location was uncertain, I decided I would rather get airborne as quickly as possible while the 'comrades' were still friendly. I'd take my chances by flying west toward either Zimbabwe or perhaps a less military looking landing field. The armed men seemed quite prepared to let us go and we were back in the warm embrace of Juliet India Papa when a farm tractor pulled into view further down the runway, with an official looking man riding on the fender next to the driver, shouting instructions to the comrades-in-arms.

The group leader came around to my door and with signs that were easily understood, indicated that we should both get out. My heart sank, and I breathed a silent prayer.

It turned out that the man riding on the tractor was the regional commander of the army in this area and a ranking officer in the country's army and ruling communist party, Frelimo. He asked for our passports, in Portuguese, but we understood and handed them over. He had a right-hand man with him who appeared to be smart and influential, so I invited him around to the pilot's seat and tried to indicate with gestures and grunts that our instruments were defective. After some communal efforts at interpreting my message, they indicated that we should walk with them. The tractor left on its own, the commander making it clear that I should walk alongside him. The comrades, who had seemed to be so relaxed up to now, sprang into action and set up a flanking escort on either side of us as we walked through the bush toward the buildings in the distance.

We tried to communicate in English and German, but to no avail. The smart young right-hand man, who it turned out later was the political commissar of the base, fell in beside me and talked to the commander as we walked. He also felt the need to explain to me the reason for the comrades' flanking escort and did this by pointing to the surrounding hills saying, "Bandidos, bandidos." He also pointed back at the plane and once again said, "Bandidos" while making a sound with his mouth like an explosion. I got the message and glanced around to look at her sitting there on the runway. I truly wondered if I would ever see her again.

As we walked, I could see the reason for the commander's arrival on a tractor. About every 50 yards along the road, there was a military vehicle of one type or another showing clear outward signs of a violent and sudden end. They had all been blown up! As we walked along I suddenly got a bit of inspiration and to nobody in particular, I said a few words in the universal pidgin language of Zimbabwe, which I had learned to speak as a child. The right-hand man lit up and promptly replied to me in the same vernacular. I was elated. Now I could explain everything and did so with great speed, shaking his hand at appropriate intervals as is customary, and enjoying his genuinely warm responses. He translated for the benefit of the commander and I could see by their softening expressions that they were somehow approving of the story. Werner, who did not understand a single word of all this, nodded agreement and smiled generously every time I looked pleased.

We soon arrived at the 'garrison,' which was no more than a group of colonial Portuguese buildings that were all much the worse for wear. There was hardly a square foot on any building that did not have bullet and shrapnel holes in it. The place was an inhabited ruin, and these guys were supposed to be on the winning side! We were ushered into a dimly lit room in one of the side buildings and told to sit down. The Commander took up the most official looking position, the right-hand man appropriately stood to his right and sundry other petty officials crowded in for what was to be a four-hour interrogation. It began in pidgin but after about half an hour a small thin man came into the room and introduced himself to us, in good English, as a teacher. He was now the official interpreter.

I immediately found out that we had landed at the Frelimo garrison of Fingoe, which was the regional headquarters for the military and civilian authorities. It was also the place in Mozambique most under attack from the rebels. I was asked for the registration of our aircraft as they obviously wanted to radio the information through to their superiors in a place called Tete, to find out what should become of us. The difficulty we faced with this otherwise simple matter was that at that time it was alleged that South Africa was supporting the rebels against Frelimo, and we had a South African-registered aircraft. Without missing a beat, I believe with divine assistance, I gave the registration but conveniently omitted the second letter, which would make it appear to be a Zimbabwean machine.

"Zulu Juliet India Papa," I announced and saw the Commander hand a note to his radio operator.

Hundreds of questions were asked about all sorts of things to establish our bona fides, and we answered clearly and directly, emphasizing that we were doing missionary work. Werner whispered to me that he had worked in a Mozambican city in the south with a well-known man and would like to mention his name. I agreed, and Werner told his story. The commander's face turned as sour as old milk in a heat wave and he interrupted the story to declare that he knew the man well and that he was a traitor. It took us about an hour to get some credibility back after that one. At this stage, time was slipping by and we genuinely had no idea what the outcome was going to be as absolutely no one knew where we were or what a terrible predicament we were in.

The first ray of hope came when the commander, who seemed to interest himself only in me, asked whether it was possible for me to fly to Harare right now. I replied that it was, but that because of the instrument failure that had brought us here in the first place, I would not be able to fly in the dark and that we would need to get airborne by 4:30 pm at the latest that same afternoon. While this was true, I had dropped that piece of information in to try and speed up our departure, if in fact there was going to be one at all.

Much discussion ensued and then they all got up and left Werner and me in the company of the translator and the leader of the group who had 'welcomed' us at the airstrip. I could see that he was very interested in my charts and no doubt saw advantages in procuring them for his own use. I wondered what else he would end up with and whether I would have any further use for them anyway. I spoke in German with Werner and asked him if he was ready to walk through the bush to Tete, about eighty miles, if we could somehow make a break for it from here. He wisely rated that one as a non-starter because of the war going on all around us. Despite the commander's question about flying to Harare, the situation looked very gloomy. I could see that the sun was getting low. Very shortly we would be stuck here even if they released us, because I would not fly at night in this part of the world even if the directional gyro was working, which it was not.

In due time the commander returned with the right-hand man and the two of them seemed to switch into official mode to address us. I braced myself for bad news. The commander began by asking me to confirm that I could not fly after 4:30 pm. Although a bit surprised at this seemingly irrelevant question, I confirmed that this was correct. I was further puzzled to see him visibly relax on hearing this and then his whole demeanor changed. He cleared his throat and then announced, via the interpreter:

"We have been in radio contact with our headquarters in Tete and they have spoken to Harare. Everything is OK and you are free to leave but we know that it is now too late. We apologize for that, but you will be my guest here until tomorrow morning when you can fly again."

I was flabbergasted and I quietly thanked the unknown person in Harare who had not 'blown the whistle' on my intentional registration omission, for they surely knew about it as we were by then a missing aircraft on an international flight plan. The leader of the group of comrades announced to me, through the interpreter, that he would personally take charge of guarding Juliet India Papa to ensure that the rebels did not 'smash it to pieces' in the night. As we found out later, this was by order of the commander and on pain of death.

Then the fun began.

The commander, who had referred to me throughout the proceedings as 'The Pilot,' now said that Werner and I would be his personal guests in the big house across the yard, but he apologized in advance for the attack of the rebels which happened most nights. I couldn't believe that I had heard correctly, but one look at the expression on Werner's face told me that I had. We thanked him, and all rose to walk over there together, clutching our overnight bags. The place was in terrible condition, with just a few sticks of broken furniture in the once grand front room of the old house. We were shown our room, which was positively huge and completely empty except for two wire cots without mattresses and of doubtful structural integrity. We both noticed the bullet holes in the window panes. This promised to be quite a night.

The interpreter announced that we would meet with the commander in the front room in 10 minutes, but he failed to say what this meeting would be for. More interrogation, I presumed. We sat in chairs which were spread so far apart in the huge room that we could hardly talk to each other and had to project our voices in a theatrical manner. The commander came in and sat down, waving his hand in the direction of a servant who quickly returned with a bottle of some exotic looking Portuguese liquor and some glasses on a tray. When we had all three been served, the commander said something and knocked his glass back, swallowing the lot in one gulp. Not wanting to offend our host and still not being too sure of the outcome of this whole adventure, I decided to do what he had done. Up went the glass, down went the liquid, and I instantly felt as if a whole football team had just kicked me in the chest. I swallowed hard, blinked back the tears and croaked a wheezy "Thank you."

The commander looked pleased and waved his hand at the servant again, but I turned the next one down, saying that as a 'pilot' I needed to be fresh in the morning. This struck the very heart of our commander who apologized profusely for his unforgivable lapse of memory in this regard as he, above all others, should have remembered this. And now the truth came out.

Our commander had wanted to become a pilot in the air force but for reasons that were not given, he was not successful. He still cherished the idea that pilots were the highest form of human life and were to be treated as such. From then on, I had to make every decision, whether it was time to eat, if we should have fish or eggs, or when to go to sleep. "The pilot must say," was repeated every time. And perhaps most significantly of all, the excellent runway that we had landed on had never been used by an aircraft before. This explained the uneducated cattle, but the commander had prepared it in the fond hope that someday an aircraft would land at Fingoe, and here we were. I found out later that there was not another airstrip for 100 miles in any direction. I call that Divine Intervention.

We were treated like kings and offered everything that they had, which was precious little. All I had to say was, "I like this tea," and packets of tea would be brought in for our journey and for our family back home. Forgetting this fact, I wanted to be polite concerning the fish that was served and presto! We had five huge salted fish for the journey in the morning. Their aroma was reminiscent of a fish market at the height of summer, but I accepted them graciously and wondered if we would ever get the smell out of our clothes.

The evening came to an abrupt and early conclusion with the somewhat practical announcement that all the lights would be going out soon because the 'time of attack' was approaching. Werner and I turned in, taking note again of the bullet holes in the windows and walls of our room and joining together for a short but earnest prayer. The night passed without incident, although we did not do much sleeping.

The day began early with the leader of the comrades banging on our bedroom door at 5:30 am, eager to announce that the aircraft was still intact. After breakfast, and eager to get going, because up until now I was still not convinced that we would actually get away, Werner and I wanted to show our genuine appreciation of their hospitality, so sacrificially given. I called everyone together, and we proceeded to give gifts to all concerned from our personal belongings. While nothing special, they were like gifts of gold and silver to these men, a pen here and a penknife there, but I saved the best for last.

Calling the leader of the comrades forward, I announced to all that because of his excellent service in protecting our beloved aircraft, I wanted to present him with a Swiss Army knife and a flight chart. I was not sure whether I could be accused of aiding their war effort by giving him a map, but seeing as he didn't even know which way Zimbabwe was, I felt that there was little likelihood of an international incident developing over this one. He beamed from ear to ear, as much for the gift as the public acknowledgement.

We were loaded on a trailer behind the faithful farm tractor and driven down to the airstrip with the whole garrison following on behind at a smart pace. As we rounded a corner and Juliet India Papa came into view, my heart literally raced a little. Pre-flight checks were made and more speeches given while Werner and I donated the remaining items in our pockets, and then the time had come to leave. The commander came forward and pointed to the surrounding hills once again saying, "Bandidos, bandidos." He pointed at me saying, "You pilot," then making his hand into a little airplane by extending his pinky and thumb in opposite directions, he indicated the preferred departure route from this valley by moving his hand along horizontally, then abruptly taking it up into a vertical climb.

I got the message.

We climbed into the plane, I woke her up for our most critical departure yet, and we were off with a roar and a cheer from the gathered comrades. I held her nose down to build up speed and then performed the most rapid climb-out that any Maule has ever achieved. It would have made Mr. Maule proud.

We were climbing through 8,000 feet on course for Harare and still on the frequency of the previous day when I keyed the mic to hear if the radio was on. Instantly, the earphones burst into life with a question.

"Is that Zulu Sierra Juliet India Papa?"

It was the Zimbabwean air force who had been out searching for us since the previous day.

Informed by the airliner of our problem, the powers-that-be in Harare had calculated that the changing weather, which we knew nothing about, had drifted us easterly into Mozambique. They knew from our relayed report that we were going to land but their information was that ALL landing strips in northern Mozambique were mined. They assumed, when the airliner could not contact us again, that we had landed and met with disaster.

I gave the pilot of the military jet our position and he flew over to verify it, asking if we were alright and whether we could reach Harare. On hearing that all was fine, he handed us over to Harare approach control and said goodbye. On the way to Harare International Airport, I did what was customary for us, and flew low over our house in a suburb of Harare, revving the engine a few times to get my very worried wife's attention. After a very scary, prayerful night, at least I could let her know that I was on my way home.

After we landed, we were asked to taxi to the customs holding area and a delegation of aviation and security officials came out to meet us. On hearing the story, they all expressed amazement that we had not been beaten up and robbed but had been treated so very well. I had to fill out a form explaining the cause of the problem and to justify the great cost of the air force searching for us.

Their official inspection of the interior of Juliet India Papa was quite brief however – due to a very strong smell of decaying fish!

PART 3

The God of Miracles

"Let there be life", said God, and what he wrought
Went marching past in myriad lives and brought
This hour ...This quiet room ... my small thought
Holding invisible vastness in its hands.

Siegfried Sassoon

CHAPTER 10

- Impact with a passing planet
- A voice in the wilderness
- From death knell to life bell

There's a saying that often comes out of my mouth, concerning witnessing about Jesus: "The man with an experience is never at the mercy of a man with an opinion."

If I could go back in time and talk to the young man I once was, a young man firmly entrenched in skepticism and unbelief, I might say exactly those words to him. Because I have *become* the 'man with an experience,' an experience of God's love for me personally, and of His mighty power to heal and restore. I know that He really is Jehovah Rapha – God who heals us – because I have experienced His life-saving restoration in my own body, and more than once!

I can't tell you why the Lord stepped in to save my life. Some people have said that the Lord must have healed me because He still has work for me to do, but I disagree and for this reason:

God's relationship with us is not as though we were chess pieces that He moves, favors and protects in the measure that they are useful to Him, but His relationship with us is one of 'unmerited favor,' which is grace, and He does what He does for us without us deserving any of it. That includes our salvation.

Impact with a passing planet

I've been an active and enthusiastic hang glider pilot for many years now, 40 to be exact, and during this time I've enjoyed hundreds of hours of incredible sights and experiences – but also one or two accidents.

The worst took place on the 9th of October 2002.

I was hang gliding in Florida, and because there are no mountains from which to launch there, the standard way of getting a hang glider airborne is to be towed to altitude by an ultralight aircraft. I had been rated for this activity and had completed hundreds of trouble-free launches using this method.

But on this day, there was some discussion about the launch technique required for the high-performance glider I was about to fly, coupled with a crosswind component in the wind. I was set up with my glider on the wheeled dolly that would carry me and the glider until there was sufficient airspeed to fly, at which time the hang glider and tow aircraft would get airborne, leaving the dolly on the ground. All did not go according to plan however. For some reason, I felt that the speed for flight had already been reached and passed, but my glider and I were still trundling along, firmly on the dolly.

I decided to release from the dolly and get airborne, but on release, the glider did not fly immediately. It bumped over the front of the dolly and sank to the ground. When it touched the ground, it stopped instantly, but as I was still attached to the tow aircraft, I was pulled into the now-stationary glider, and my head collided with the airframe.

I lay amongst the wreckage, still fully aware of what was going on and immediately realized I could not move my legs at all. I knew then that I had broken my neck.

Emergency services were called while I lay very still in the shade of my glider. I asked someone to hold a cellphone to my ear, and I spoke to Evangeline. I wanted her to know what was happening, but much more than that, I couldn't help but remember the dear friend of hers who broke her neck in a car accident. Although she lived on for many years as a quadriplegic, she was never again able to speak another word. My thoughts at that moment were that if I was never to speak again then the one thing I wanted to say now to the love of my life was, "I love you."

When the paramedics arrived, I loudly informed them that my neck was bad. They tried to cut off my flying harness, but that proved impossible and the plan was changed. A gorilla of a man in the paramedic team just lifted me up bodily while the harness was removed, and I was installed in the ambulance. On arrival at the nearest emergency hospital, an x-ray was done of my neck, and the doctor on duty gave me the sobering report.

"Your neck is broken," he said, "but we cannot help you here and will send you by helicopter to the place that handles the difficult cases."

My heart sank, and I wondered what the future held for me as I tried to move my unresponsive legs and tingling toes. But right then, called on by Vangi, our ministry colleagues, family and friends around the world began to pray.

I arrived by helicopter at a hospital in Orlando, Florida, not far from where we lived, and there I met Evangeline for the first time after the accident. We held hands and prayed quietly.

I was informed by the hospital staff that it 'just so happened' that the leading neck and spine surgeon in Florida was here at the hospital on a visit from Miami, and that he would look at my case. When I heard this, I immediately saw it as the 'finger of God' at work miraculously for me. The surgeon said that I had broken three vertebrae in my neck, numbers five, six and seven, and that the bone was displaced by 40% into the spinal column. (You can see the MRI for yourself in the photos section.) None of this gave hope for a good outcome, but God was at work!

I was prepared for the surgeries, as there were to be two, and when the anesthetist was about to inject my arm and put me to sleep, I said to him, "Hold it! I need to speak to the surgeon."

I could see him in the next room in operating scrubs, sterile gloves already on. He was called to my side.

"Doctor," I said, "I'm a Christian and because of the work that we do, there are thousands of people around the world praying for you right now." Then I quickly added, "And for me too!"

He nodded his head and I went to sleep. When I awoke, the surgeon was there, and he informed me that the prayers seemed to be working, because the first operation had gone very well. He added that he would do the second one in 24 hours.

The second operation went well too, and I was sent to intensive care for the first two days of recovery. While I lay in bed with all sorts of monitors checking me out constantly, I kept trying to move my legs, holding onto the idea that I desperately needed them for launching my hang glider. I practiced and exercised them continually as I felt the beginnings of feeling returning.

During this time in the ICU, I received a phone call from Reinhard, who was in India at the time and had just received the news that 'Pete has broken his neck'. On the long distance call he began by saying, "Pete, what happened?"

I told him that it was a hang gliding accident and then he said, "I want to pray for you."

Those were the last words he said because he began to sob and sob over the phone, unable to gather himself to speak. After a while, I interrupted his sobbing, myself in tears, and said,

"Reinhard, that is the best prayer I have ever heard, and I accept it fully!"

After just four days in the hospital, I was able, with nervous assistants hovering nearby, to walk around the ward unaided. Over the next few days, this resulted in a never-ending parade of hospital staff coming into my room and asking me to walk for them. I commented to the nurse that she sure had a lot of staff on this floor, to which she replied that they were not her staff, but people from the whole hospital who had seen the MRI scan of my broken neck and could not believe that just four days after the operation, I was walking. I knew it was the hand of God and said so to anyone who was inclined to listen.

Only nine days after the surgery, sporting a huge and solid-looking neck brace and with instructions to lie on my back for weeks, I left the hospital with my beloved wife and daughter, who had flown out from South Africa to be with us.

Not long after this, we transferred my convalescence to our home in South Africa where we traditionally spent Christmas with our children and grandchildren.

I grew rapidly stronger, so much so that a mere eight weeks and three days after the accident, I was able to remove my neck brace and fly a hang glider again. I said that I would foot launch from the hill and land quickly on the beach, just to show myself that I could still do it. I did launch but felt so comfortable that I remained airborne for an hour, landing on the beach after that with a huge smile on my face.

Once again, the hand of God had made all the difference.

A voice in the Wilderness

It was the year 2012, and 10 years had passed since the accident in which I had broken my neck. I am an active person by nature and I have been very active in hang gliding again since my rapid and full recovery. I'm also an advanced Scuba Rescue diver, I ride a mountain bike, and enjoy extreme off-road driving and river kayaking, so being fit and energetic has always been a part of my life.

But early that year, I began to have feelings of fatigue, aching joints and general malaise. It was most uncharacteristic for me. It took a while before I realized that it was not a passing problem but something that was getting worse and worse. Eventually, with an increased heart rate, tingling in my toes with numbness, loss of balance, horrific shingles and the feeling that my life's energy was slipping away, I went to see the doctor.

He wanted to treat the symptoms, but I was convinced from what I had read that the root cause was that my immune system was under attack. He then referred me to a renowned infectious diseases specialist in the area who had a six-week waiting period for new patients.

I called the expert doctor and told him that I was leaving shortly for Nigeria and Cameroon and that I needed his help before that. Amazingly, he asked me to come to him the next day, which I gladly did. Many blood tests were done and then I returned to him for the report. He read the results and looked up at me, surprise on his face.

"What do you for a living?" he asked.

"I'm a missionary to Africa," I replied.

"How often do you go there?" he asked. I replied that we went there eight or nine times a year for weeks at a time.

"How long have you been doing this?" was his next question and I told him it had been about 40 years. He shook his head and said,

"You have been exposed to every imaginable disease and your viral load is so high that it's now suppressing your immune system."

He said that the only thing to do was to prescribe daily anti-retroviral drugs, which I would have to take for the rest of my life.

With this information and clutching the newly acquired drugs, we left for our usual Christmas break in South Africa where I routinely participated in a lot of hang gliding and particularly in a competition. But this time I was too weak and unwell to do so, and so I joined up with the organizer of the event to assist him where I could.

During the hang gliding competition one day, we took a break for lunch. We left the restaurant in the village of Wilderness to return to the launch site by car. I was in full outdoor mode, roughly dressed and covered in dust, traveling in the passenger seat of the vehicle, when we came to a stop sign in the center of the village. Imagine our surprise when suddenly, a man came striding boldly right across the intersection towards us and pounded on the driver's closed window with the instruction,

"Wait!"

He then marched around the front of the vehicle, coming to my window, which I had opened slightly.

"What is your name?" he asked.

I quickly replied "Joe!" not wanting to give my name to a crazy man in the street.

"Are you a minister?" he asked.

"Yes!" I answered.

"Are you in a position of authority?"

"Yes!"

"I have a word from the Lord for you," he said. Immediately I shouted that my name was Peter, not wanting the word of the Lord to go to 'Joe.' He just kept talking.

"You have had a tough year, but the Lord says that you will not die but you will live and do His work. This year ahead will be your best year ever!"

Then he turned and walked briskly away. I shouted after him, "Thank you for being obedient to the Holy Spirit!" but he never even looked back. I turned to look at the other two men in the vehicle. There was a stunned silence as they stared back at me, because they were amongst the few who knew how very ill I was.

One of them asked me if I knew that man. I said, "No, I've never seen him in my life."

The other one, also a pilot and a believer, just sat there mumbling, "Jesus, Jesus, Jesus!"

To say we were all stunned is to seriously understate the matter, but in that moment, I knew that God cared about me and my problem. My heart and spirit soared and from that second, I never looked back physically, going from strength to strength and indeed beginning the 'best year ever'.

That night I related this incident to Evangeline and we rejoiced together. Then, just a few days later, an amazing confirmation came to light through a visit with a friend from the village who had come for coffee. She was the widow of a former high-ranking politician from the apartheid era, and during their visit she related this story.

She told Evangeline that someone had asked her if she could give a few days' accommodation to a pastor and his wife whose accommodation plans had not worked out during this busy Christmas time. Although a very private person and not accustomed to sharing her home with others, she felt that it was the right thing to do. She then related, almost in passing, an interesting thing that had happened to her guests a few days before. She said that as they walked through the village of Wilderness, the husband told his wife that he had a word from the Lord for 'the man in the passenger seat of that vehicle' at the stop street. His wife admonished him to not just stand there but go and give it to him, and he did, crossing the intersection to give the message.

Evangeline interrupted her friend to say, "That man was my husband, Pete, and the message was straight from the heart of God for him!"

How amazing are the works of the Lord on our behalf! He is speaking all the time and all we have to do is to listen and obey. The encouragement that this episode gave me was a good foundation for another trial that was just around the corner.

From death knell to life bell

The phone rang unexpectedly at 8am on the day before Evangeline's birthday and a very agitated doctor's voice crackled in my ear. It was the oncologist I had visited the previous day because of a lump forming in my left eye socket.

"Your diagnosis is not as expected," he said. "It's Burkitt's Lymphoma!"

I responded that I didn't know exactly what that was, but since he was calling me at home so early in the morning, it had to be bad!

His quick reply was, "It's a very aggressive form of cancer that is known to spread rapidly throughout the body and to grow tumors at a very fast rate. I have spoken with a leading authority on Burkitt's who is at Shands Cancer Hospital in Gainesville, Florida, and they are expecting you there. Go to Emergency and check in. The oncology staff will meet you there."

Half in shock, I said I understood, but when should I go there? He raised his voice urgently:

"You must go now! Right now! As soon as we finish this call you must get there as quickly as possible."

It had started some weeks before on a ministry trip to Germany and Africa, when I noticed a slight swelling in my left eye. Thinking it was a stye or something similar, I was not alarmed at all. But it continued to grow until other team members kept asking what the problem was. By the time we returned to Florida, the eye was 80% closed, suffering double vision, flashing lights and shadows, plus a loss of focus, so I immediately went to an ophthalmologist.

He was not unduly alarmed, thinking that it was a common, benign tumor that could be removed surgically, and I was booked for the procedure. As is normal practice, the surgeon cut my eyelid open to reach the tumor but before removing it they did a biopsy, which showed positive for cancer. He stitched the eyelid closed and I was referred to an oncologist, whose first assessment was that it was an 'orbital lymphoma' that would respond well to radiation. He booked me for the radiation and more tests, but said there was a section of the original biopsy pathology that he still had not seen. He wanted to check that first.

This resulted in the revelation of Burkitt's Lymphoma and his urgent phone call the next morning that changed everything.

I asked a friend to drive me the two hours to Shands Cancer Hospital as I was obviously going to be admitted, and while I waited for him to arrive, I went online to find out more about this 'Burkitt's Lymphoma.' And find out I did! I learned that it was indeed a rare and very aggressive form of cancer known for a high fatality rate, especially in Africa, with a known characteristic of spreading rapidly throughout the body, spinal fluid and bone marrow. I noted that nobody over the age of 60 had ever survived it. I was 68 years old at the time and I knew that I had been handed a *death sentence*!

Both my wife and I were shocked to the core, and we immediately jumped into action by informing everyone that we could think of about the crisis and asking them to pray. I also handed all my computer ID's and passwords over to her and we set in motion the sale of a second property that we owned to simplify our financial world, given the strong likelihood of my imminent demise.

I arrived at Shands Hospital Emergency and was admitted to Ward 8 East, a well-known cancer ward. Many intensive tests were carried out during the day, including scans, X-rays, ultrasounds and multiple blood tests.

In the meantime, the bad news went out far and wide to our colleagues in ministry and to many friends and family around the world, asking them to pray. Due to the public nature of the work we do, this resulted in hundreds, perhaps thousands of people joining us in prayer for the desperate situation.

The pathology showed beyond doubt that it was Burkitt's Lymphoma. Chemotherapy would start immediately. It was to be the most extreme regimen possible, with the shortest recovery time between sessions. I was politely and sympathetically informed that there were many side effects to this extreme treatment that would make me very sick in many ways. Being familiar with regular chemotherapy as witnessed from the experience of friends and family, I had some idea of what to expect. Further browsing online confirmed that the side effects would be extreme, some long-lasting, while others could even be fatal.

At this stage, I was asked by my daughter what it felt like to receive a diagnosis of aggressive cancer with a poor prognosis. She reminded me that this was *her* asking, my very frank daughter Tanya, and that she did not want to hear the sanitized version. I gave it thought and responded from my heart.

"It has been a great shock to both your mother and me," I replied, "shocking us to the depth of our being, because in our society, the word 'cancer' is regarded as synonymous with sickness and death. But despite this I have an inexplicable, deep, calm confidence inside me that is NOT dependent on staying alive. It doesn't sound reasonable to my enquiring mind, but it is still there, deep and strong, and I know it is the work of the Holy Spirit in me because I don't have that capacity naturally."

The chemotherapy began with seven powerful chemicals, some of them deadly. Some were being given to me orally but most intravenously. I readied myself for the drama ahead – and promptly fell asleep! I woke later to find that I had absolutely no bad effects from the initial hours of chemo and this was the first indication that something good was going to happen. My beloved Evangeline told me that she had been praying that my case would be 'atypical' – and it had started.

As the week of continuous chemotherapy progressed, it became more apparent by the hour that I was doing very well so far, with no adverse side effects at all. I even refused the anti-nausea tablets because I didn't need them. Most amazing of all was the fact that the tumor in my left eye, large enough to touch my glasses and close the eye completely, started to shrink dramatically and was completely gone in just three days. The chemotherapy was working very well indeed, and one nurse commented that this was 'unusual.'

After the 100 hours of continuous infusion in the first session were over, and I was still feeling great, well-meaning personnel warned me that, after coming off the drips and going home for the two weeks of recovery, I would certainly feel sick. The opposite happened. I was able to fill my ministry role for three days the very next week at our School of Evangelism in Orlando. I told the delegates that I was not supposed to be present as I was meant to be dying, and they gave me a standing ovation!

I was back in the hospital for the second five-day session of chemo two weeks later and thanks to the many prayers, the session was going just as well as the first time. No adverse reactions and no nausea – both very unusual, as I was told continually. Despite the predictions that I would definitely be sick *this* time, there were still no side effects at all, even though some of the seven powerful chemicals being poured into me were actually poisonous and very unfriendly to human flesh. This was made clear on the chemical pack itself, which instructed nurses to wear boots, tunic, gloves and face masks when handling the substance. I asked, tongue in cheek, where *my* protective clothing was, as the fluid dripped into my veins.

During the first chemo session three weeks previously, they had drilled a hole in my head and fitted something called an Ommaya reservoir. It is a little rubberized bulb that is fitted under the scalp skin and has a pipe that goes through a hole in the skull, and down between the brain lobes into the base of the brain where the spinal fluid is produced. The idea is to get chemicals into the bulb by injection. These then go directly into the spinal and cerebral fluid to fight cancer in that area (a common destination for Burkitt's cancer, resulting in brain tumors, a real possibility in my case because of the obvious tumor in my nearby left eye). At the same time, they withdrew some spinal fluid to test for cancer cells and the wonderful result received was that it was negative! This is what we and so many others had prayed for.

There were smiles all round. Once again, we could see the hand of the Lord at work and the nurse who called my situation 'unusual' during the first session now upgraded her observation to 'amazing!'

I went home again for two weeks to recover and still the much-predicted sickness never materialized. However, on my return for the third session, I had some feelings of trepidation. This time, even though I was still embarrassingly well, I could sense that there was a build-up effect going on inside me from all the poison bombardment so far. But I was told they would do tests after this session to see what the present state of the cancer was. If there was none, we would hold a 'Thank you Jesus!' party.

When I arrived in the cancer ward for this third five-day chemo session, a really moving thing happened. Many nurses and orderlies came from all around to say 'hi,' smiling and laughing and shaking my hand. I commented that their patients must all look forward to coming back to such a reception. They whispered that this didn't usually happen, because others were 'depressed or angry and bitter about being here ... But you are different.'

I replied that it wasn't me, but Jesus in me. HE was making all the difference.

Did I mention that from the second session onwards, I had so much energy that the staff brought me a fancy exercise bike, which was placed in my room? Each session, I climbed random hills for a total of around 35 miles. I'm sure it was an odd sight – a man in that strange hospital gown with the ventilated posterior, pedaling like a madman with infusion pipes flying up and down from his drip tower.

And still no side effects at all, prompting the nurse to upgrade her observation yet again, this time to 'incredible!'

It was apparent now to any observer that something extraordinary was taking place in my case, and all the time I was eager to point to Jesus as the one answering prayer, even though I, myself, really could not explain exactly how that works. The longer I progressed without side effects, the more and more others began to acknowledge that God was at work.

By Saturday morning when I was about to leave the hospital after the third five-day chemo session, I felt better than I had after both the previous sessions, and I decided to drive myself home from the hospital in my open Jeep. One doctor heard about this and told me, shaking his head in disbelief, that he had never had a five-day chemo patient drive themselves home, even around the corner, never mind for two hours. I simply smiled and said to him that Jesus was unquestionably at work!

These reports were sent out to the many people praying, with the addendum to 'keep it up because your prayers are working!' That was no publicity stunt, but simply passing on what we were witnesses to day by day.

The ninth week came.

Between the third and fourth chemo sessions, I had a PET scan, the results of which would reveal the extent of the cancer and guide further treatments.

The next day, I got a phone call from the main doctor's assistant, giving me a summary of the report. I think it's significant that I received the call while out playing 18 holes of golf in a charity challenge. The best way I can convey the message I received that morning is to give you the doctor's exact words, remembering that doctors do not easily speak in superlatives or absolutes.

"I'm calling to give you a summary of the report on your PET scan from yesterday. It's a very good report. A very, very good report. Even the radiologist said that this is a great scan report." Then he went on to say, "The disease is not totally eradicated, but it's very close. A very good report!"

He then wished me well on my upcoming mission trip to Africa and said they would see me when I got back.

I couldn't help but be reminded that the last phone call we had received from a doctor on this subject had been just nine weeks previous, and it had been tantamount to a death sentence. This whole process to that point in time can best be described by the nurse, who upgraded her observation yet again and said, "You are a miracle in progress." And we give all the glory to Jesus.

Before the next chemo session, I went to Blantyre, Malawi (in central Africa), to preach in the Fire Conference and to be a part of the whole event as usual, which I did without any problems or sickness at all. I preached my full share alongside Daniel Kolenda, and at the end of it, I felt, happy, grateful, privileged, and not even tired! Not bad – considering that I was supposed to be in chemotherapy that whole week. Amazing? Yes, Jesus was at work!

Right after returning from the event in Malawi, I travelled back to Gainesville and Shands hospital, this time for the fourth chemo session. I met immediately with the leading doctor for a review of the recent PET scan. The scan showed, as I had suspected, that the cancer could not be seen anywhere. I was told that usually for lymphoma cancers, when a clear PET scan was attained, they would do one more session to be sure. But the doctor said that with Burkitt's Lymphoma, there was no data on doing less than the full six sessions. She talked with a colleague and looked at other data, then said that she recommended doing the present session, number four, and then one more to complete. (That's five in all, and from what I could gather, this had never been done before with Burkitt's.) It really was miraculous!

At the end of the fourth chemotherapy session, when the team of doctors saw me, they reiterated that all my blood work and tests were perfect, and then instructed me to have a photo taken downstairs standing next to the huge 'Total Remission

Bell' and to post it online. I questioned whether this should be done before the final chemo, and one of them answered, "Yes, because the scan is already clear and the final session is now only prophylactic."

There were smiles all round as this is not the usual speech given to Burkitt's Lymphoma patients who are over 60 years of age.

Needless to say, our hearts were full of joy and gratitude to our Savior for His intervention on my behalf. I've said to many that I don't really understand how prayer works, but I am a beneficiary and a witness to its effectiveness. And so is everyone else who has observed this incredible process!

Evangeline and I went downstairs together to ring the 'Total remission bell.' It was a very emotional moment indeed, and I took the wooden club provided and struck the bell so hard that it nearly burst our eardrums! Through the ear-splitting noise, with a broad smile I said to her, "This is the sound of *life*!"

I left soon after for our campaign in Tema, Ghana (in West Africa) and as you can imagine, I was really looking forward to it with my whole heart.

Immediately on my return to Florida, we drove the two hours back to Shands Cancer Hospital in Gainesville and met with the professor who headed up the team working on my case. She looked at all the records again, turned to me and said,

"Your case has exceeded all our medical expectations!"

She commented to another doctor present saying, "I have never had a case like this in my life. It has been extraordinary."

Then the professor came out from behind her desk to wrap us both in a big hug, and there wasn't a dry eye in the room.

All these amazing comments are directly attributable to the tremendous work of the medical team at Shands Cancer hospital and of course, to the incredible and miraculous intervention of God through prayer. I thank the Lord for making my case 'atypical' as my beloved and many others so often prayed.

During the last few days of the fifth and final chemo session, many nurses and medical personnel, who were not caring for me directly at that time, came to my room to greet me and acknowledge that my case was amazing and miraculous.

The gravity of what had transpired was brought graphically home to me when one nurse came in after her shift, and on hearing something of the latest reports, she said that she wanted to give me a hug, but that her scrubs were contaminated by other patients. She promised to come back in the morning with clean scrubs on, and to give me that hug. She did so, and said she had been on this cancer floor for two years and that I was the fifth Burkitt's Lymphoma case in that time – and that I was the first one to leave. Not only that, but I was leaving early! When I questioned this, she explained that the other cases had the five months with six sessions, then kept returning after some months for another six sessions. She added that one patient would not be returning but would be moving to a hospice. This gave me a fresh perspective, and I looked at her and said, "It really is miraculous, isn't it?" – to which she simply nodded her head and with teary eyes, gave me another big hug.

This is the fingerprint of God! He is at work, and I am an amazed but grateful beneficiary.

From a death sentence to the sound of life, by God's grace.

PART 4

Before I go ...

Then I heard the voice of the Lord saying, "Whom shall I send? And who will go for us?"
And I said, "Here am I. Send me!"

Isaiah 6:8

CHAPTER 11

The Third Identity

Any activity in life that involves others apart from yourself, which is practically everything, requires an approach that is initially not so obvious.

Whether it be a romantic relationship, a relationship with others inside an organization, or in a family group, our behavior and attitude to the relationship is vital to its success. A bad attitude, no matter how well justified, will spell the end of the relationship. Many people who go through this come out of a broken relationship – romantic, work or ministry related – as 'right' but alone or excluded. Just speak to any such person who has walked that path and you will always hear how very justified they were. My view is that the best result in any and all relationships is not the perceived correctness of my standing, but the survival and good of the relationship itself, if you attach any value at all to that relationship.

Let me explain it from our own experience.

As you've read, Evangeline and I, together with Oliver Raper, began Rufaro while we were still in Bible College. We were, and still are, three strong personalities with strong ideas of our own. This sounds like a formula for conflict, given that we worked and lived together 24/7 and had integrated finances in order to survive. Yes, there were differences of opinion and varying ideas on where and how the ministry should progress. But I soon realized that when we sat together to settle these differences and perhaps to persuade each other of our personal point of view, there was another entity present amongst us. That entity was the ministry itself, Rufaro. And I saw in myself and the others, that each of us was prepared to settle for solutions that were not altogether what any of us wanted, but which were best for the ministry, Rufaro.

I then realized that with my marriage to Evangeline a very similar situation had already been established. When we disagreed on something and discussion began, I was aware of a 'third entity' present that obtained consideration from me and Evangeline. Not a person, but our marriage. And many times, we agreed to do something that was not her first choice, or my first choice, but clearly the best choice for our marriage.

This also applies to ministry situations when, very often, we end up following a directive that is perhaps not the best for us individually, but best for that unseen but ever present other entity – the ministry. In our case, that ministry is Christ for all Nations.

In this way, it is possible to share a vision and a calling by submitting in service to someone else's vision. I often say, "We haven't all been called to be the number one, the leader, the top dog!"

This may appear to be self-evident, but all the same, many people in ministry see themselves as filling a lesser role, until they eventually reach the top position of leadership. As a result, they are in a permanent state of transition and never give themselves fully to their current role, nor reach full effectiveness in what they are doing, always thinking of what might be in the future.

In real and practical terms, there just *must* be more workers or team members than leaders. The old adage still holds true of many organizations, especially in the Christian world, that there are often, 'too many chiefs and not enough Indians!'

The truth is that the call of God in a person's life can be to many and varied roles and not only to leadership in ministry. CfaN is a practical demonstration of this, with a very high percentage of our team worldwide fulfilling technical and administrative roles that are far from the preaching platform but crucial to the success of the whole ministry. They are called of God and work tirelessly above and beyond the call of duty to see the harvest brought in. Truly, their reward is in Jesus' hands and we know what His view of this is.

I have no doubt at all, from my own experience, that God honors such an attitude. Those who lift themselves up will come to ruin, but those who are 'servants of all' will prevail. (Matthew 20:26-28)

Jesus Himself is our great example.

Where could the Call of God take me?

Many of us get stuck on this sobering and challenging question.

As a young couple way back in 1974, when we felt ready to answer the call of God, we didn't know the answer to this question at all. But it didn't matter. What we did know was that we felt we had been directed by the Holy Spirit, and what we wanted most of all was to follow His leading no matter what.

Even the stern words from the college dean in the USA, that we were irresponsible to think that we could go to Bible school with three very young children, did not deter us. Yes, where this was heading was a mystery, but as Evangeline likes to say,

"I have learned to love the mystery."

From then on, we simply got on with the program as it unfolded before us. I was trained all my life as an engineer. On top of that I had, and still do have, a skeptical philosophical view on many things. But now, for the first time, I was stretching my wings into the unknown, learning to ride the wind of the Spirit!

Bible College was a revolution for us both. I went from years of mathematics, science and engineering, to find myself steeped in Greek, Hebrew and historical theology. And I was expected to understand it and give it back in exams.

For Vangi, she was a young mother and new wife, but she suddenly found herself thrust into a different culture and student world, with children displaced from their home and grandparents. On top of this, she was called upon to contribute her obvious talents to training and leading the college choir.

Did we pull back, or appeal to others to set our financial or study priorities? No, we didn't, because we saw every single opportunity as part of the call of God for us as individuals and a family.

You have read in this book how we developed into a music group, into leadership in college and then saw the birth of a music-based evangelistic ministry. More was to follow: ordination, the joy of seeing many giving their lives to Jesus across the UK, then joining Christ for all Nations, then under the leadership of Reinhard Bonnke.

The years with CfaN have been the same. Many – perhaps sometimes *too* many – responsibilities appeared and were embraced. I never turned one down because of the knowledge that I was in this position through the call of God, and as Jesus said,

So likewise you, when you have done all those things which you are commanded, say, 'We are unprofitable servants. We have done what was our duty to do.' (Luke 17:10 NKJV)

The call of God is like that for all of us. He waits only for our agreement and commitment, and then He, by the Holy Spirit, does the rest. That's why we cannot accept the praise and glory for any of it.

It is all God.

I am convinced that if you say *yes* to the call of God in any form, you will begin, as we did, the most exciting and fulfilling journey through life that any human can experience. No, it is not without problems and challenges. The Word of God promises us many, but it also promises us that He will be with us in and through them all.

By God's grace, we are witnesses to this fact.

The Crisis of Faith

I have been asked many times how we kept our faith strong throughout the many changes and adjustments that 45 years of ministry presented – five different countries of permanent residence and three different citizenships. The following Bible story and illustration have both been fundamental to our understanding of God's dealings with us. I believe they can work for you, too.

In the Old Testament book of Ezekiel, chapter 37, the prophet recounts his vision where the Spirit of the Lord placed him in the middle of a valley that was full of dry bones. As he stood looking at the dryness around him, obviously not a pleasant or potentially productive situation, he must have wondered, as we often do too, why he was in this problematic environment. When God asked him whether the bones could live, he was quick to say, "O Lord God, You alone know."

We certainly can identify with Ezekiel's situation and that is a good place to start. He must have been overwhelmed by the very obvious problem around him, but the word of the Lord came again, powerful and strong. "Prophesy to these bones, and say to them, 'O dry bones, hear the word of the LORD! THUS SAYS THE LORD GOD to these bones: "Surely I will cause breath to enter into you, and you shall live." (Ezekiel 37:4-5 NKJV)

Here lies the crunch! The good news is that dry bones can live. The bad news is that it depends on our obedience. We *want* to hear God's word for our situation, but so often we would prefer or expect to hear someone else speak the word of life over us and our problems. Ezekiel may well have had the same preference, but the Lord clearly and emphatically told him that HE should speak life to the dry bones.

The dilemma that Ezekiel faced in this moment was what I call a 'Crisis of faith.' Should he speak the word of the Lord in his situation or should he wait for someone else to do it? Should he believe and speak or should he assess and review the problem? He was facing a crisis of faith and would not see or experience the power of God at work in his situation until he somehow went through this crisis of faith.

The way to go through the crisis is to speak the word of the Lord in and to your own situation. This is what we as Christians are called to do; to speak God's word into our own lives and into the lives of others. This could be a declaration of salvation, or a claim for healing or a pronouncement of deliverance. The list goes on. But the key is that nothing will happen until you and I 'speak the word of the Lord' and go *through* the crisis of faith.

I love the following story that I heard many years ago while still at Bible school. I have used it many, many times because it illustrates this truth so vividly.

A man was on a long journey by foot through a dry desert land. In the parching heat, he soon used up his water supply but he kept on walking in the hot sun. Without water and with the sun burning fiercely, he felt his energy diminishing with every step, but he pressed on bravely. He grew weaker and weaker until finally, all he could manage was crawling on his hands and knees. He realized that he desperately needed water soon or he would die. He knew there was a watering hole ahead and with a last, mighty effort, he gathered all his remaining strength to reach it. On arrival at the oasis, he saw an old, rusty water pump, half buried in the sand. He crawled up to it, he brushed the sand away and stood shakily to his feet.

With what remained of his strength, he took the handle of the pump and began pumping, but all he got was a dry, rusty, squeaking sound. His heart sank. Then he noticed a small bottle of water lying on the ground near the pump and his spirits rose a little. He thought to himself that even though it was not much water, he would drink it and live for one more day. Picking the bottle up, he saw that it had a note attached to it with this message. "To make this water pump work, take this bottle of water and pour it into the top of the pump. When you push the handle, you will receive water from the pump. When you have drunk your fill, please fill the bottle and leave it for the next traveler."

Now what was he to do? Should he drink the water in the bottle or should he believe the words on the note? What if it was a cruel joke? He faced a crisis of faith, exactly as Ezekiel faced in the valley of dry bones, and exactly like you and I face every time that we want to see the power of God in action in our own situations. Ezekiel only saw the hand of God at work after he spoke the word of God to the dry bones and our experience has been the same. Every time we faced a desperate, challenging or difficult situation, personally or in the ministry, speaking the word of God directly or in prayer, made the difference every time.

Let me return to the story of the man at the water pump. Like Ezekiel, he didn't hesitate but acted on the word. He poured the water into the top of the pump and eagerly pushed the handle up and down. At first, he still only heard the dry, rusty squeak, and he felt a twinge of fear. What had he done? Had he been foolish to believe the word on the bottle? Had he missed a chance of survival by exercising faith? Then the handle grew heavy in his hands as he pushed against the resistance, and before long, what he now heard was the gurgle of an imminent miracle! Glorious, refreshing water gushed out, more than enough for him to quench his desperate thirst and even enough to bathe in. He had gone through the crisis of faith. Gratefully, he refilled the bottle and put it where the next traveler would find it. He also knew that if he ever came that way again, he would once again have to exercise his faith in the words on the bottle, but now he was informed by experience.

For Ezekiel, it was the same. He spoke the word of God for that situation, and the bones began to move around. Flesh and skin appeared on them, and before long the prophet was surrounded by the bodies of men lying on the ground. It was a mighty miracle, but still not complete.

He had to speak again to complete the miracle. This time he was told to prophesy to the four winds to come and breathe on the bodies around him and reveal their true potential – a living, breathing army!

This continues to be our experience. Every time we need to see the power of God in action in our lives and situations, we face the crisis of faith which we can only go through by speaking God's word, over and over again, for as long as it takes to complete the work. And let me encourage you with this – the more you face a crisis of faith and go through it, the easier it becomes!

Can anyone know the call of God?

The answer to this question is a resounding 'YES!' To know the voice of God and have the opportunity to follow it, you first need to know Him.

This is made possible by God Himself, who has opened His heart to all mankind in an amazing gesture of grace – 'unmerited favor'. Even though we deserve retribution for our sins, He made a plan for us to be set free from them all and to appear before Him without guilt.

How does it work? The death of Jesus paid the price in full for you and me and cancelled our debt. All you need to do is believe it and receive it.

After that, you begin a new life as a follower of Jesus Christ, and your own spirit becomes alive to the Holy Spirit of God. This laid the foundation for me and millions of others to hear and follow the call of God.

I make no apology for encouraging you to do the same, knowing that like me, you too will be launched on the greatest and fullest adventure of life – following Jesus.

ABOUT THE AUTHOR

Born in Zimbabwe, then Rhodesia, in 1947, Peter, his wife Evangeline and their three children traveled the world, from South Africa to the UK to America. After seven years of evangelistic ministry with the Gospel group Rufaro in the UK, he joined Evangelist Reinhard Bonnke at Christ for all Nations in 1981 where Peter currently serves as Executive Vice President of CfaN, helping to plan and manage hundreds of open-air evangelistic campaigns as well as ministering the Gospel message.

For more information visit PeterVandenberg.org

Peter and Evangeline's
wedding day 1969

Blantyre-Malawi -
Preaching during chemotherapy

Hang gliding above the beach

Blue Grotto Dive
July 2016

Flying High in California

Getting ready to go in the Maule

Joining CfaN 1981

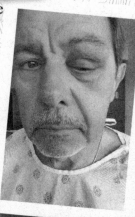

Eye tumor just before
commencing chemotherapy

A typical CfaN campaign meeting with
750,000 people present

Peter flying over the sea

Ringing the 'Remission Bell' at
Shands Cancer Hospital

Broken neck 2002

Titanium neck parts 2002

Rufaro in the city hall,
Birmingham, England 1980